# Genocide?

# GENOCIDE?

## *Birth Control and the Black American*

ROBERT G. WEISBORD

JOINTLY PUBLISHED BY

*GREENWOOD PRESS*

*Westport, Connecticut* ● *London, England*

*THE TWO CONTINENTS PUBLISHING GROUP, LTD.*

*New York, New York*

**Library of Congress Cataloging in Publication Data**

Weisbord, Robert G
    Genocide?   : Birth control and the Black American.

    Bibliography:  p.
    Includes index.
    1.   Birth control—United States.   2.   Negroes.
3.   Genocide.   I.   Title.   [DNLM:   1.   Family planning
—United States.   2.   Negroes.   HQ766.5.U5 W426g]
HQ766.5.U5W33   1975          301.32'1          75-13531
ISBN 0-8371-8084-8

Library of Congress Catalog Card Number: 75-13531
Greenwood Press ISBN: 0-8371-8084-8
Two Continents ISBN: 0-8467-0069-7

First published in 1975

Greenwood Press, a division of Williamhouse-Regency Inc.
51 Riverside Avenue, Westport, Connecticut 06880

Trade distribution in the United States by The Two Continents
Publishing Group, Ltd., 30 East 42 Street, New York, New York 10017

Printed in the United States of America

In Memory of Grandfather, Samuel Guberman

# Contents

# *Acknowledgments*

In the preparation of this book I have incurred numerous debts. I am especially grateful to my friend and colleague, Leon Bouvier, who encouraged me to undertake this study. His prodding and his critical comments were most helpful. Another friend and co-worker, Joel Cohen, read the manuscript and made several useful suggestions. To Abner Gaines, Bill O'Malley, Carol Winn, and Kathleen Schlenker of the University of Rhode Island Library I am deeply indebted for their efforts on my behalf. Graduate assistants Tom Goodrich, Richard Kazarian, Edith Merman Beckers, and Joe Ritzo, are also entitled to a vote of thanks. Others who aided in various ways were Tony and Avril Bryan, Ed Cahill, and Everett Lee. Julia Hoxsie, Lorraine Randall, Kathie Hendry, Betty Hanke, and Debbe Carter contributed their secretarial talents. A grant from the Ford and Rockefeller Foundations Program in Support of Social Science and Legal Research on Population Policy made some of the initial research possible. I would also like to express my appreciation to Betty Gonzales of the Association for Voluntary Sterilization and to Frederick Jaffe of Planned Parenthood for making their files available to me. Portions of this work are contained in "Birth Control and the Black American: A Matter of Genocide?" *Demography*, November 1973. Without the forbearance of my wife, Cynthia, this book would never have been completed. Without the interruptions of my dear but indefatigable children it would have been completed much sooner.

# Genocide?

# 1. Birth Control as Black Genocide—Fact or Paranoia?

In the last few years there has been much global concern about overpopulation and its deeply disturbing consequences: famine, the depletion of natural resources, and pollution of the environment. The year 1974 was designated "World Population Year" by the United Nations. It also organized an international conference, held in 1974 in Bucharest, Rumania, to confront new and terrifying demographic realities. The United States was an active participant in the parley.

For decades contraception, abortion, and sterilization were subjects considered too coarse for polite conversation in American society. They were practices that were often legally restricted, even proscribed, in this country. Times have changed. It is no longer necessary to whisper furtively about birth control. Information about family planning and actual planned parenthood services are now lawfully available. Birth control has come of age.

Success was not easy for the birth controllers to realize. Like the tortuous road leading to racial equality, their path was narrow and winding. There were potholes and roadblocks galore. Martin Luther King once spoke of the striking kinship between the civil rights movement and the early birth control movement, both of which he said were aimed at alleviating horrible slum conditions.[1] Margaret Sanger, founder of the birth control movement, just as Dr. King many years after her, nonviolently resisted unjust laws and was jailed. Like the meetings of abolitionists a century earlier, public gatherings sponsored by the proponents of birth control were frequently prohibited or disrupted. For decades, knowledge of efficient contraceptives was the monopoly of the rich. Poor people were not allowed to share the secret of family size limitation. It was against this gross inequity that Margaret Sanger, undaunted by her formidable opposition, waged her courageous crusade.

Legal hurdles confronting the fledgling family planning movement were seemingly insurmountable. Tariff laws enacted in the latter part of the nineteenth century banned the importation of contraceptives along with abortifacients and a whole list of "immoral" items and "obscene" materials. The same prohibition was contained verbatim in the 1930 Hawley-Smoot tariff passed during the ill-starred Hoover administration. An 1873 law inspired by that paragon of puritanism, Anthony Comstock, secretary of the New York Society for the Suppression of Vice, had barred from the United States mails "obscene, lewd, lascivious, filthy and indecent materials." Contraceptives and literature about conception prevention were included in the ban. A highly effective means of disseminating her birth control views was thus denied Mrs. Sanger. Who would then have guessed that in the 1970s the United States postal system would posthumously salute that gallant lady by issuing a family planning postage stamp?

Anti-birth control laws were ruthlessly enforced. Mrs. Sanger's pioneer clinic in the Brownsville neighborhood of Brooklyn was raided by the police in 1916. She was arrested and convicted of violating Section 1142 of the penal code of New York State which said, in effect, that no individual or group could distribute contraceptive information to anyone for any reason. Her sentence was thirty days in the workhouse.

Arrayed against the birth controllers was the might of the

Roman Catholic Church to whom Mrs. Sanger, the daughter of a renegade Catholic, was almost the devil incarnate. Archbishop Patrick Hayes of New York pronounced contraception a more heinous sin than abortion: "To take life after its inception is a horrible crime; but to prevent human life that the Creator is about to bring into being is satanic." Abortion at least allowed the soul to survive, but prevention of conception denied the immortal soul existence in time and in eternity. [2] At that time, orthodox Jews, conservative Protestants, and the Greek Orthodox concurred with the Roman Catholics about the inherent wickedness of contraception.

Never a revolutionary breed, medical practitioners were not to be found in the vanguard of Margaret Sanger's birth control crusade. By and large they were indifferent at best and antagonistic at worst. With some physicians religious scruples were a restraining force. With others it was contempt for a lay woman who was encroaching upon their professional terrain. Cowardice in the face of federal and state anti-contraceptive statutes silenced the voices of still others. In a celebrated incident which Margaret Sanger recalled in her autobiography, a poor woman's entreaty to a doctor for contraceptives drew the crude response, "Tell Jake to sleep on the roof." On that occasion the woman, Mrs. Sadie Sachs, a mother of three living on New York's lower east side, had almost died following a self-induced abortion. [3]

"Neutrality," that is, neither approval nor disapproval, is how the American Medical Association characterized its posture on family planning adopted in the 1930s. Yet its House of Delegates in 1936 disapproved of lay bodies that spread propaganda regarding the control of conception. In retrospect, it can be seen clearly that the "neutral" stance of the AMA was nothing less than dereliction of medical duty. The AMA admitted as much in 1964 when it revised its policy on what it called a very important medical-socioeconomic problem. Its new stand was that "the prescription of child spacing measures should be made available to all patients who require them, consistent with their creed and mores, whether they obtain their medical care through private physicians or tax or community-supported health services.''[4] Better late than never.

Prior to 1958 New York City's twenty tax-supported municipal hospitals had an unwritten law on prescriptions for contraceptives. Even advice about contraceptives was withheld from the impoverished patients to whom these hospitals catered. Dissatisfaction with this antediluvian policy had long festered. In July 1958 it finally erupted: in a case involving a diabetic woman whose life was endangered by a future pregnancy, the commissioner of hospitals expressly forbade the fitting of a diaphragm. The ensuing dispute was protracted and bitter and led to a reversal of the New York City hospitals' posture on contraceptive prescriptions. In the informed judgment of Dr. Louis Hellman, that victory marked a turning point in Americans' attitude toward governmental distribution of birth control information.[5]

Dwight Eisenhower once observed that birth control was not the concern of the federal government. But that observation was made when he was still residing in the White House and population was a prickly issue to be avoided. Ex-President Eisenhower completely reversed his stand when he came to realize that the population explosion was smothering economic growth around the world and was threatening international peace. Choosing the number of children individuals will have was a right which governments had to secure both in the United States and abroad, he came to understand after taking his leave from political life.

By the 1960s birth control had been popularized by the introduction of the pill. Sexual attitudes became increasingly permissive. Whether a ''sexual revolution'' was actually underway is debatable, but undoubtedly public policy regarding family planning was radically changed. In June 1965 the United States Supreme Court invalidated an 1879 Connecticut statute which outlawed the use of contraceptives by any persons, even married couples. The court ruling established a ''right of privacy older than the Bill of Rights.''[6] Litigation challenging the archaic Connecticut law had resulted from the arrest of two leaders of Planned Parenthood in Connecticut. They had been convicted and fined

$100 each for operating a birth control clinic in New Haven. In March 1972 the high court overturned a Massachusetts law prohibiting the distribution of birth control devices to single persons.

Birth control, it seems, has become generally respectable. Since the early 1960s American presidents have openly professed a concern about population problems. Both Republican and Democratic party platforms in 1972 contained planks explicitly calling for expanded voluntary planned parenthood services. On a somewhat limited scale federal moneys now finance family planning services and population research. Almost four million American women in just about every section of the country were the beneficiaries of family planning assistance provided at government expense during a twelve-month period ending June 30, 1973. This figure is expected to rise to six and a half million by 1975. Government-subsidized birth control clinics are springing up with incredible speed. The statute books of a dozen states still contain laws curbing the circulation of family planning information, but their constitutionality is doubtful. Moreover, according to a mid-1971 public opinion poll, 90 percent of all Americans believe that such information should be made available to men and women who want it.[7]

While family planning is desirable to a large part of the American public, sections of the black community as well as other minority communities view it with distrust and/or disdain. Amid the mushrooming debate about the dangers of unchecked population growth, specific allegations have been made that birth control programs constitute a thinly disguised white plot to commit genocide against people of African extraction in the United States and elsewhere. This idea is frequently voiced in the black community. Glaring differences and divergencies exist in the thinking of black Americans on this controversial subject so that one generalizes at his peril. The declaration by a white New Leftist that Afro-Americans regard population control "with unusual unanimity . . . as just another approach to their extermination"[8] is false and misleading. Blacks do not speak with a single voice on population issues, but with many voices. For that matter they rarely speak with one voice on any issue.

It is fair to say that most, but certainly not all, of those who are vocally apprehensive about birth control being genocidal are identified with black nationalist or black revolutionary organizations. In general, the more estranged from the U.S. government blacks feel, the greater their misgivings about the motivation behind planting birth control facilities in black neighborhoods are likely to be. Discussion of contraception, abortion, and sterilization is usually passionate. On at least one occasion black fulminations against birth control have been translated into violence: a family planning clinic in Cleveland was burned by arsonists actuated by the conviction that planned parenthood meant genocide for Afro-Americans.[9]

Ordinarily, however, the fervent opponents of birth control are content to make their case in the marketplace of ideas. In speeches and articles they decry the evil motives of white birth controllers and the dangers inherent in black acceptance of birth control. There has even been a very brief one act play written to spotlight the menace of birth control. Entitled "Top Secret Or a Few Million After B.C.," it was written by the black author, Ben Caldwell. The President of the United States, two generals, and three cabinet members comprise the entire cast. Caldwell's scenario follows. Concerned about the problem of surplus "niggers" who are responsible for social disturbances, the president seeks a final solution more subtle than but just as lethal as that advanced by one army general, i.e., killing them off. No black babies, a reality to be achieved by birth control, is the answer decided upon. The plan is simple. Unsuspecting blacks ever ready to model their behavior after that of whites would be sold the idea of what is to be euphemistically branded "family planning." Blacks would be told that their poverty was the result of their having too many children. Having fewer offspring would enable them to have sports cars and color television sets. "Negro leaders" were to be used to dupe ghetto blacks unaware that in one generation there would be a "nigger shortage" so acute that there could not be a march on

Washington. Riots, if they materialized, could be suppressed by the Boy Scouts. An ecstatic president orders a crash birth control program along these lines. It is to be given a priority even higher than that given to the space program. Money is to be no object.[10]

Of course, there are less conspiratorial expressions of the genocide fear. In a speech delivered in 1968 to a liturgical conference in Washington, D.C., Floyd B. McKissick seemed ambivalent about the demography of blacks. Shortly before McKissick's talk, Pope Paul VI had issued the encyclical, *Humanae Vitae,* reaffirming the traditional Catholic opposition to physical and chemical contraception. McKissick, who was on leave of absence from his post as national director of the Congress of Racial Equality (CORE) at the time of his speech, found fault with the Roman Catholic hierarchy for being impervious to the social problems of the poor caused by overpopulation: "It is all too easy for the Pope to say that Black people don't need the pill." Simultaneously, McKissick criticized many white Protestants for thinking that birth control is a panacea for the problems of poverty: "If poor people and Black people just stop having children, the whole problem will go away. In a few more generations, there will be no more poor people and no more Black people—they seem to conceive of birth control as a sort of painless genocide." McKissick went on to warn his audience that such an approach was doomed to fail. Black people loved babies. They would resist being told by welfare or church agencies how many children they should have. They would demand freedom of choice insofar as their own fertility was concerned. "It is the decision of the individual Black person, as it is of the individual white person, to determine if he wants children and how many children he wants to have," McKissick insisted.[11] This viewpoint, that family planning should be available to people but not foisted upon them, is commonly stated by black spokesmen.

Since McKissick's speech, the best publicized black pronouncements on birth control have generally tended to be more intemperate. They have tended to put forward a more unequivocal genocide interpretation. Why? Is the "birth control equals

genocide'' theory based on fact or fiction? Are black fears of birth
control rational and justified, or are they reflections of paranoia?
Qualms about conception control are inextricably bound up with a
more generalized dread of genocide. Is this foreboding evidence of
nothing more than black delusions of persecution? The main
purpose of this book is to supply some answers to these questions
by examining the roots and rationale of the genocide school of
thought, with particular reference to birth control.

## NOTES

1. Martin Luther King, Jr., *Family Planning—A Special and Urgent
Concern* (New York: Planned Parenthood—World Population, n.d.),
pp. 2-3.

2. Quoted in Margaret Sanger, *Margaret Sanger—An Autobiography* (New York: W. W. Norton and Company Publishers,
1938), p. 308.

3. Ibid., pp. 89-91.

4. *Journal of the American Medical Association* 190 (21 December
1964): 31-32.

5. Louis Hellman, "One Galileo Is Enough: Some Aspects of
Current Population Problems," *The Eugenics Review* 57, No. 4
(December 1965): 161-166.

6. *Griswold et al.* v. *Connecticut*, 381 U.S. 479 (1965).

7. Gerald Lipson and Dianne Wolman, "Polling Americans on Birth
Control and Population," *Family Planning Perspectives* 4 (January
1972): 39.

8. See the Foreword by Steve Weissman to Ronald L. Meek (ed.),
*Marx and Engels on the Population Bomb* (Berkeley: The Ramparts
Press, 1971), p. xix.

9. *New York Times*, 15 November 1968.

10. Ben Caldwell, "Top Secret Or a Few Million After B.C.," *The
Drama Review* 12, No. 4 (Summer 1968): 47-50.

11. Speech by Floyd McKissick to the Liturgical Conference, Park
Sheraton Hotel, Washington, D.C., 20 August 1968.

# 2 . The Meaning of Genocide

Before proceeding, certain terms must be clarified. For purposes of this study the terms *birth control* (a term initially coined by Margaret Sanger), *family planning,* and *planned parenthood* will be used synonymously. All may be defined as "voluntary planning and action by individuals to have the number of children they want, when and if they want them."[1] On the other hand *population control* is used to connote the belief that for the good of society in light of overpopulation individuals and groups should reduce the number of children they produce. Semantic confusion necessitates a very careful examination of black pronouncements to determine the intended meaning. Perhaps the confusion is inevitable in view of the sensitive nature of the subject.

It is imperative that the precise meaning of *genocide* also be understood. Genocide is defined as "the use of deliberate systematic measures (as killing, bodily or mental injury, unlivable conditions, prevention of births) calculated to bring about the extermination of a racial, political or cultural group or to destroy the language, religion or culture of a group."[2] Essentially, this dictionary definition is based on the United Nations Convention for the Prevention and Punishment of Genocide, although that agreement speaks more broadly of the intent to destroy a group "in whole or *in part*" (emphasis mine). An effort to eradicate a portion of a people thus qualifies as genocide insofar as international law is concerned. An act of genocide need not entail a bid to murder every man, woman, and child in any group. However, the term has usually been applied to grisly episodes of wholesale butchery.

Genocide is a new word in the English language, having been coined toward the end of World War II in response to Adolph Hitler's demonic policies aimed at annihilating Jews. Since that dark era the word has been applied variously to the mass atrocities committed against the Ibo people during the Nigerian civil war of the 1960s; the massacres of Bengalis by Pakistan in Bangladesh's struggle for independence in 1971; and the killing of untold thousands of Hutus by fellow Africans in Burundi in 1972.

Blacks have long accused white Americans of trying to annihilate Americans of African descent. Family planning, they feel, is just another means to this end joining the political oppression, economic exploitation, and outright brutality of earlier epochs. An historic petition leveling the grave charge of genocide against the United States government was presented to the United Nations in 1951. Several years afterward the dynamic black revolutionary, Malcolm X, also prepared a petition for presentation to the world body, charging this country with genocide against twenty-two million black Americans.

For racial and other reasons the United States has never officially subscribed to the UN's genocide convention. The Senate's failure to ratify the compact first submitted to it for approval in 1949 is a stain on our national honor. It is morally inexcusable. For twenty-five years opposition to the convention has been led by southerners and their allies who jealously guard United States sovereignty. In the words of the *New York Times* their attitude betrays "a heavy burden of guilt for past mistakes in the treatment of minorities and an appalling lack of faith in the progress that has been made, particularly in the South, toward righting past wrongs."[3] During the 1974 debate over ratification, Senator Peter H. Dominick, Republican of Colorado, speaking in opposition to ratification, raised the possibility that some day birth control clinics might be construed as contravening that section of the pact which includes within the meaning of genocide "imposing measures intended to prevent births within the group."[4] A political conservative, Dominick, who lost his Senate seat later that year, was quoted approvingly by black separatists opposed to birth control.

Birth control has actually formed one element in the overall genocide indictment, and it is crucial to appreciate the fact that negative black attitudes toward planned parenthood do not exist in a vacuum. They are a central part of the whole sweep of black history. To fully grasp the inclination of some Afro-Americans to equate birth control with a genocidal campaign against them, it is necessary to comprehend what the late Malcolm X meant when he quipped: "We didn't land on Plymouth Rock. It landed on us." In other words, it is necessary to acknowledge the grim realities of the history of black-white relations, a history which antedates the Pilgrim landing in Massachusetts. It is a history which, until the 1960s, was usually ignored, glossed over, or distorted. When the unvarnished truth is clearly presented, it reveals that for centuries blacks have repeatedly played the role of anvil to the white role of hammer.

Even a cursory examination of the racial drama shows how low a premium has been placed on black life. Act one commences with the slave trade. Luckless Africans en route to enslavement in the New World endured the infamous and inhuman Middle Passage across the Atlantic. Chained like wild animals, the Africans on the slave vessels were fed a monotonous, unbalanced diet which left them susceptible to a variety of diseases, smallpox and flux among them.[5] Because of overcrowding, the slave had little room to move about. Sanitary facilities, when they existed at all, were wholly inadequate. Female slaves were fair game for the crew, particularly the ship's officers. Incredible brutality was exhibited toward the black cargo. Insubordinate captives were dealt with unmercifully. In short, the slaves were regarded as subhuman creatures and treated accordingly.

To appreciate just how ruthless the trans-Atlantic commerce in black flesh could be, one need only look at the case of the Liverpool slave ship, *Zong*.[6] In September 1781 the *Zong* sailed from the Guinea coast of Africa bound for Jamaica. Seventeen whites and approximately four hundred and forty African slaves were on board. In late November as the vessel was approaching her destination, she suddenly veered off course. Seven whites and over sixty Africans had already died. Many more of the latter were gravely ill. They would certainly be of no market value in the West Indies. Chances were they would not even survive the journey. The dead and dying slaves represented a significant loss to the owners of the *Zong*. Apparently, it occurred to the ship's captain that the potential loss could be transferred to the underwriters. If part of the cargo were jettisoned to save the rest, a claim for damages could be filed. The captain made a fateful decision to throw one hundred and thirty-three of those sickly slaves least likely to recover into the sea. Supposedly, his reasoning at the moment was that water was scarce and the slaves were certain to die anyway. Why require the poor wretches to linger a few days longer?

A trial followed, made inevitable by the adamant refusal of the insurers to pay damages. In the midst of the proceedings, John Lee, an attorney for the ship's owners, turned to Granville Sharp, the philanthropist and long-time opponent of slavery, who was sitting in the courtroom. Lee remarked to the judges that a person, not mentioning Sharp by name, intended to press for a criminal prosecution for murder. But, the lawyer said contemptuously, it would be madness because the blacks were property. Therefore, the case was one of chattels or goods, whether rightly or wrongly, it did not matter. Lee overlooked the true nature of the property in question, but in a legal sense he was correct. No indictment for murder was forthcoming. In the civil action the presiding judge, the Chief Justice Lord Mansfield, held that "though it shocks me very much, the case is the same as if horses had been thrown overboard."

Upon learning of the *Zong* incident an English clergyman called it "one of the most inhuman barbarities that I ever read of." A second divine labeled it "one of the blackest projects that ever entered the mind of man." Thomas Clarkson, the ardent British abolitionist, characterized it as a "deed, unparalleled in the memory of man . . . so black that were it to be perpetuated to future generations and to rest on the testimony of an individual, it could not possibly be believed." These observations were made in eighteenth-century England, a notably callous age. Ordinary Caucasian life was held to be of little account; the life of Africans was of virtually no account. Nevertheless, by the standards of that or almost any era, the case of the slave ship *Zong* is incredibly shocking.

Exactly how many Africans perished in the many stages of the slave trade—resisting capture, marching to the West African coast, awaiting shipment, crossing the ocean, adjusting to new surroundings during the initial seasoning period in the Americas —cannot be ascertained. Estimates of the number of sons and daughters of Africa involuntarily transported to the Western Hemisphere range from less than ten million to more than fifty million. Those who survived the ordeal of enslavement and the seasoning period may not have always been the fortunate ones.

Guilefully dubbed the "peculiar institution" by John C. Calhoun, one of its staunchest defenders, slavery was usually a heartless, sometimes a sadistic, enterprise. Bondsmen were defenseless before the wrath of their masters. On occasion abuse of the Negro slave included sadistic medical experiments. Two such occasions were related by a surviving victim. John Brown, later a fugitive who managed to make his way to freedom in England, vividly recalled incidents in his life as a slave in Georgia.[7] Once, a physician eager to find the best remedy for sunstroke used John as a guinea pig. As a slave he had to resign himself to his fate in ignorance and in much fear. A pit was dug three and a half feet deep, three feet long, and two and a half feet wide. Dried red oak bark was placed in the pit and burned until the opening was as hot as an oven. John was compelled to remove his clothes and to sit in the hole with only his head above ground. Medicine was given to him. The physician wanted to see how much heat he could with-

stand before fainting. With short intervals of a few days the
experiment was repeated five or six times. A different medicine
was administered each time to determine which would allow the
slave to tolerate the highest temperature.

Experiments were also performed on Brown to ascertain just
how deep his black skin went. Periodically, his feet, legs, and
hands were intentionally blistered, leaving indelible scars. For a
period of nine months John was an unwilling participant in these
and other barbaric medical studies. So enervated was he at the end
of that time that he was unable to toil in the fields.

Throughout the slave empire recalcitrant blacks were dealt with
harshly. Flogging was the rule, not the exception. Even pregnant
women were not spared. Branding was another means used to keep
the slaves in line. There were also masters who did not shrink from
killing troublesome blacks.

Slave narratives are full of stories of men, women, and children
who were whipped to death or shot in cold blood, often on the
slightest pretext.[8] Sometimes a slave was murdered for the sheer
perverted pleasure of it.

Sadism alone can explain a little known episode in American
history which occurred in Kentucky in December 1811. Two
brothers, Isham and Lilburn Lewis, murdered and mutilated a
black for breaking a pitcher which had been a favorite of their
deceased mother. These barbaric criminals were none other than
the nephews of Thomas Jefferson, his sister's sons. Jefferson, it is
said, could never bring himself to utter a word about the incident.
Perhaps because the uncle of the killers was a national celebrity,
the author of the Declaration of Independence, and an ex-
president, the local authorities could not turn a blind eye to what
the Lewis brothers had done. They were indicted for murder.
Lilburn Lewis died of natural causes shortly thereafter. Isham was
sentenced to death but managed to escape from jail. It is believed
that he was killed during the battle of New Orleans at the end of the
War of 1812.[9]

Slave killers were rarely brought to justice, however. For
depriving a slave of his life early colonial laws prescribed either no

punishment at all or, alternatively, a fine or short prison term. Following the American Revolution, the statutory penalties for homicide against slaves were made much more severe. However, enforcement of the new legislation was difficult. Kenneth Stampp has written of the circumstances which mitigated the murder of slaves. If death resulted from the act of correcting a slave, it was not considered homicide. Similarly, if a slave was slain while rebelling or while resisting arrest, the deed was regarded as "justifiable homicide."[10] Moreover, inasmuch as blacks could not testify against whites in courts of law, convictions seldom occurred. White racial solidarity was another obstacle to equal justice. White witnesses were reluctant to testify. White juries were loath to convict. Based on his exhaustive research, Stampp has concluded that with very few exceptions, Caucasians who were guilty of feloniously slaying blacks did so with impunity.[11]

"Sometimes a overseer kilt a nigger, and dey don't do nothin' to him 'cept make him pay for de nigger," recalled one-time chattel Henry Lewis, a centenarian when he was interviewed in the twentieth century.[12] Bondsman James Roberts has left us two bloodcurdling stories of the unpunished murder of blacks on a plantation owned by one Calvin Smith. The first involved Ben who had killed an overseer. A barrel was constructed to Ben's dimensions. Spike nails were driven through the container into which the hapless slave was inserted. The barrel was then taken to the top of a hill and rolled down. James Roberts described the gruesome consequences for Ben: "his whole body was a perfect jelly, or perfect mince meat. Every particle of flesh was torn from his bones. The cask was opened and the jelly, for his flesh was nothing else, was thrown into the river."[13]

On another occasion, Calvin Smith's son-in-law purchased a black named John who refused to accompany his new master. The defiant slave was then lashed unmercifully with a whip of wire and buckskin. He was carried to a bridge. There John's head was split open and he died. So bestial was the son-in-law that he was willing to lose the $500 purchase price rather than acknowledge the humanity of a black man.[14] It may be surmised that only pecuniary

considerations restrained many slave owners from venting their
sadistic impulses. Blacks were valuable property. Arbitrary and
capricious killings were wasteful to agricultural capitalists, which
is precisely what the slave owners were.

In the light of the subhuman treatment accorded black people by
the Constitution, such inhumanity should occasion little surprise.
For purposes of representation and direct taxation, the Founding
Fathers resolved that a black was to count for three-fifths of a man.
Floyd McKissick has not been alone in noting the staggering
implications of the three-fifths compromise devised by the constitutional convention which met in Philadelphia, the city of
brotherly love, in that unbearably hot summer of 1787. McKissick
has written: "It meant that the slave was considered less than
human, a bit more than an animal perhaps, but less than human."[15]
The intrinsic humanity of Afro-Americans remained a moot question. In its infamous Dred Scott decision handed down in 1857, the
Supreme Court held that persons of African descent were not
citizens of the United States, that they were of an inferior order,
and that they had no rights which a white was bound to respect.
Chief Justice Roger Taney was voicing the sentiments not merely
of a majority on the court but of the overwhelming majority of
Americans.

Negroes were the targets of sporadic mob violence. Anti-black
eruptions took place in Philadelphia in the 1830s and 1840s,
bringing death and destruction to those whose only crime was their
pigmentation. After colored Americans were hired as
longshoremen on the wharves of the Ohio River, Cincinnati's
black section was put to the torch in 1862. Perhaps the most serious
outburst of Negrophobia in the North occurred in New York City
during the Civil War. I refer to the so-called Draft Riots of 1863
when black people were indiscriminately beaten and lynched.
Homes and businesses owned by blacks were reduced to ashes.
Even the Colored Orphan Asylum was destroyed.

Race rioting became something of a national pastime at the
beginning of the twentieth century. The summer of 1919, in the

estimation of the estimable black historian John Hope Franklin, "ushered in the greatest period of interracial strife the nation had ever witnessed."[16] Racial explosions comparable to those which had virtually devastated Atlanta, Georgia, Brownsville, Texas, and Springfield, Illinois, some years earlier took place in the nation's capital, in Chicago, and in more than twenty other cities. Twenty-three Negroes were killed in the Chicago upheaval alone. Unlike the urban conflagrations of the 1960s, racial convulsions before the Great Depression were little more than anti-black massacres. An East St. Louis race riot in 1917 in which thirty-nine blacks and nine whites perished has been aptly likened to a Russian pogrom.

Lingering doubts about the historical willingness of whites to liquidate black Americans are easily dispelled by the unholy history of lynchings in this country. Records compiled by the National Association for the Advancement of Colored People have authenticated 3,224 lynchings during the period 1889 to 1918 inclusive.[17] Of the victims 2,522 were black. They had been accused of murder, rape, and sundry other crimes against persons and property. In some instances they were accused of nothing at all. How many were truly guilty of wrongdoing we shall never know. We do know that they were not put to death for their crimes, real or imagined. Clarence Darrow, attorney for the damned, including the black damned, explained it best: they were lynched because the Lord painted their faces black. While the vast majority of the victims were killed in the South, there were two hundred and nineteen slain in the North and one hundred and fifty-six in the West. Georgia and Mississippi had the highest lynching totals, with Texas and Louisiana not very far behind.

Bloodthirsty mobs made no distinction based on gender. They took the lives of black women, some carrying unborn babies. No fewer than seventy Afro-Americans were lynched in 1919. Some were returning servicemen still wearing their military uniforms, men who had fought for the country to make the world safe for democracy. Lynch victims were sometimes hanged, sometimes burned at the stake, sometimes both. Mutilation was not unknown. In its description of the lynching of a black farm laborer in Georgia in 1899, the *New York Tribune* wrote:

> Before the torch was applied to the pyre, the Negro was deprived of his ears, fingers and other portions of his body with surprising fortitude. Before the body was cool, it was cut to pieces, the bones were crushed into small bits and even the tree upon which the wretch met his fate was torn up and disposed of as souvenirs.
>
> The Negro's heart was cut in several pieces, as was also his liver. Those unable to obtain the ghastly relics directly, paid more furtunate possessors extravagant sums for them. Small pieces of bone went for 25 cents and a bit of the liver, crisply cooked, for 10 cents.[18]

Though their savage ritual was witnessed by an enthusiastic horde of two thousand, those responsible for the lynching were never arrested. That was a common situation. Advertised in advance, a lynching could provide an evening's entertainment for the entire family, even little children.

Why not? Minions of the law looked the other way. And elected representatives of the people gave their approval to the practice. To hell with the Constitution if it hindered the lynching of rapists, cried Pitchford Ben Tillman, the demagogic senator from South Carolina. Never reticent about defending the lawless use of rope and faggot, he told the United States Senate in January 1907 that when white men "put to death a creature in human form who has deflowered a white woman they have avenged the greatest wrong, the blackest crime in all the category of crime."

As repugnant as the killing of blacks at the hands of mindless, passionate vigilantes is, judicial murder of blacks is even more odious. There is no shortage of evidence to show that innumerable black Americans lost their lives because of the racial prejudice of our criminal courts. Indeed, there is an abundance of data to sustain the notion that harsher sentences have been meted out to blacks, especially when their crimes have been committed against Caucasians. This has been conspicuously true in the South. It has been borne out by one thorough investigation of three thousand convictions for rape in eleven states south of the Mason-Dixon line from 1945 to 1965. Only 13 percent of the black rapists received the death penalty, but that figure was seven times higher than the percentage for convicted white rapists. If the black had ravished a white woman, the chances that he would pay with his life increased very dramatically.[19] This investigation led to the inescapable conclusion that racial differentials in death sentences could not have been due to mere chance. They were the product of racial bias. Nationwide, from 1930 on four hundred and fifty-five males have been put to death for the crime of rape. All but fifty were black. Bare statistics from the Commonwealth of Virginia from 1908 when execution by electrocution was begun until the mid-1960s attest to the crass racial bigotry inherent in the judicial process. All fifty-six men executed by the state during the more than half a century in question were of African descent and were found guilty of rape-related offenses.[20] Reflecting on the number of blacks who have been executed, former Attorney General Ramsay Clark has said: "It is outrageous public murder, illuminating our darkest racism."[21]

In an historic 1972 decision, *Furman* v. *Georgia,* the Supreme Court held, five to four, that the death penalty in the cases under consideration constituted cruel and unusual punishment in violation of the eighth and fourteenth amendments to the Constitution. All three petitioners whose appeal led to the high court ruling were Afro-Americans. Two were convicted rapists, the third a convicted murderer. In his majority opinion, Justice William O. Douglas cited studies which demonstrated that capital punishment had been unequally applied to the poor, especially blacks. Douglas did not conclude that the petitioners themselves had been sentenced to death because they were black, but he wrote somewhat cynically, "One searches our chronicles in vain for the execution of any member of the affluent strata of this society."[22] Justice Thurgood Marshall, the only black member of the court, in a concurring opinion referred to studies which indicate that "while the higher rate of execution among Negroes is partially due to a higher rate of crime, there is evidence of racial discrimination."[23]

Racial discrimination is not confined to the question of capital punishment. It is intrinsic to the entire criminal justice system and may determine who will be apprehended, who will be indicted, who will be convicted, what the verdict will be, and how severe the sentence will be. A black judge in Los Angeles recently commented that since slave times "blacks have received the butt end of justice."[24] To our everlasting shame as a nation, the historical record bears him out.

Vital statistics are also grist for the rhetorical mill of the genocidal theorists. Mortality among blacks has plummeted since the last years of the nineteenth century. On the average a life span of twenty-five years was all that the black female born in 1880 could expect. Life was short, sordid, and brutish. Life expectancy for a black female born in 1970 is approximately sixty-seven years. However, the more crucial statistic is that white females still live seven years longer than blacks in the United States. Death rates for black Americans are significantly higher than for Caucasian Americans at all ages. There is, for example, a flagrant racial disparity in infant mortality. The black rate in 1971 was almost double that for whites.[25] Racial discrimination is clearly a matter of life and death.

Poverty has forced many blacks to eat a less nutritious diet and to dwell in more overcrowded, unsanitary homes. Compared to whites their medical care is very inadequate. Bluntly put, living in unlivable conditions, blacks do not live as long. No deliberate, systematic program, designed and orchestrated in the White House or on Capitol Hill, has brought about this cruel inequity between the races in what we never tire of boasting is the richest nation in history. Rather it is the inevitable result of decades of pervasive racism. One may speak of governmental apathy or societal neglect. Some talk of genocide.

## NOTES

1. This was proposed as a definition of "family planning" to the National Family Planning Forum in Chapel Hill, N.C., on 9 and 10 March 1972.

2. *Webster's Third New International Dictionary of the English Language, Unabridged* (Springfield, Mass.: G. & C. Merriam Publishers, 1964), p. 947.

3. *New York Times,* 7 February 1974.

4. *Congressional Record,* 5 February 1974, S 1265. Dominick also stated that forced school busing and low welfare benefits have been mentioned as possible genocidal acts.

5. Daniel P. Mannix and Malcolm Cowley, *Black Cargoes: A History of the Atlantic Slave Trade* (New York: Viking Press, 1962), p. 107.

6. *Gregson* v. *Gilbert.* Henry Roscoe, *Reports of Cases Argued and Determined in the Court of King's Bench (1782-1785)* (London: S. Sweet and Stevens and Sons, 1831) 3: 233-234. For the complete story of the *Zong,* see Robert G. Weisbord, "The Case of the Slave Ship *Zong,*" *History Today* 19 (August 1969): 561-567.

7. John Brown, *Slave Life in Georgia* (London, 1855), pp. 45-48.

8. B. A. Botkin, *Lay My Burden Down—A Folk History of Slavery* (Chicago: University of Chicago Press, 1958), pp. 12, 55, 164, 179.

9. This incident is the subject of Robert Penn Warren's gripping play, *Brother to Dragons.*

10. Kenneth Stampp, *The Peculiar Institution* (New York: Vintage Books, 1956), pp. 219-220.

11. Ibid., p. 222.

12. Norman R. Yetman (ed.), *Life Under the "Peculiar Institution": Selections from the Slave Narrative Collection* (New York: Holt, Rinehart and Winston Inc., 1970), p. 205.

13. James Roberts, *The Narrative of James Roberts* (Chicago: Printed for the Author, 1858), p. 25.

14. Ibid.

15. Floyd McKissick, *Three-Fifths of a Man* (New York: The Macmillan Co., 1969), p. 56.

16. John Hope Franklin, *From Slavery to Freedom: A History of Negro Americans* (New York: Vintage Books, 1969), p. 480.

17. *Thirty Years of Lynching in the United States 1889-1918* (New

York: National Association for the Advancement of Colored People, 1919), p. 7.

18. *New York Tribune,* 24 April 1899.

19. Marvin E. Wolfgang and Marc Riedel, "Race, Judicial Discretion and the Death Penalty," *Annals of the American Academy of Political and Social Science* 407 (May 1973): 119-133.

20. Donald H. Partington, "The Incidence of the Death Penalty for Rape in Virginia," *Washington and Lee Review* 22 (1965): 43-75.

21. Ramsay Clark, *Crime in America* (New York: Pocket Books, 1971), p. 313.

22. *Furman* v. *Georgia,* 408 U.S. 252-253.

23. Ibid., 364.

24. *New York Times,* 19 February 1974.

25. *Monthly Vital Statistics Report Annual Summary for the United States,* 1971, Vol. 20, #13, 30 August 1972 (Rockville, Md: U.S. Department of Health, Education and Welfare, 1972).

# 3 . *Black Sexuality and*
# *the Racial Threat*

Although the whole of black American history comprises the backdrop against which the genocide fear has evolved, white manipulation of black sexuality in particular has fed nervousness about birth control. Sexual exploitation has done the black family great injury. Anger is often generated among Afro-Americans when the black family is talked about; witness the heated and protracted argument over the "Moynihan Report."[1] No wonder. In slave days the Negro family was a precarious institution which existed at the sufferance of the master. It could be and sometimes was dissolved at the whim of a callous owner. "Husbands" were parted from their "wives," young children from their parents. Heartrending tales of loved ones sold separately, never to be reunited, were not contrived by abolitionists. Monetary considerations often preceded humanitarian ones. This is not to say that slave family units were typically torn asunder, but it did happen and not just once in a while.

Not infrequently slaves were mated as if they were livestock. Thomas Dew, president of William and Mary College and a rabid proponent of the slave system, took pride in the fact that Virginia was a Negro-raising state. Historian Frederick Bancroft wrote that, "Next to the great and quick profit from bringing virgin soil under cultivation, slave-rearing was the surest, most remunerative and most approved means of increasing agricultural capital."[2]

"Breeding slaves," "child-bearing women," "too old to breed" were everyday phrases in the vocabulary of the slavocracy. Male slaves were sometimes set up as stallions and certain slave women with proven or anticipated fecundity were deemed especially valuable as "breeding wenches." Conversely, barren slave women commanded comparatively low prices at the auction block.

Aided by a storehouse of statistics, Robert William Fogel and Stanley L. Engerman, cliometricians or "new economic historians," have lately challenged the traditional view that systematic breeding of blacks for sale in the market was a lucrative practice. Whether profitable or not, slave-raising went on. It was not the norm on the antebellum plantation, but several slave narratives attest to the fact that breeding was not a figment of the anti-slavery imagination.[3]

Frederick Douglass, the remarkable black abolitionist who had himself been born a slave, recalled the case of a poor white man, Edward Covey, who had purchased a black woman as a "breeder." The woman, Caroline, was twenty years old and had already borne one child. Covey then mated a hired man with her with the expectation that there would be issue. After a year, much to her master's delight, Caroline produced twins. The children were a significant addition to Covey's wealth. A revolted Douglass commented that the slaveholder was no more condemned for buying a slave for breeding than "for buying a cow and raising stock from her, and the same rules were observed, with a view to increasing the number and quality of the one as of the other."[4]

Elige Davison, an ex-slave, remembered his master mating him with about fifteen different women. He was certain that he had fathered in excess of a hundred children. Katie Darling, who had been born into bondage in Texas, succinctly summarized the breeding custom: "massa pick out a p'otly man and a p'otly gal and just put 'em together. What he want am the stock." Another chattel born in the Lone Star state, Jeptha Choice, was interviewed in the twentieth century about the not so good old slave days. He recollected: "The master was might careful about raisin' healthy nigger families and used us strong, healthy young bucks to stand the healthy nigger gals. When I was young they took care not to strain me and I was as handsome as a speckled pup and was in demand for breedin'."[5]

James Roberts, who entered the world on the eastern shore of Maryland as a piece of property, has provided us with a nauseating account of the breeding and selling of mulattoes. Lighter skinned Negroes fetched higher prices on the market than their ebony-hued brothers and sisters. On the plantation of the notorious Calvin Smith fifty to sixty "head of women" were kept for reproductive purposes. Only whites were permitted access to them. Twenty to twenty-five racially mixed children were produced annually on the Smith plantation. Roberts told of a second planter who competed with Smith in the breeding of mulattoes "the same as men strive to raise the most stock of any kind, cows, sheep, horses, etc."[6]

Jordan Smith, a surviving ex-slave, was interviewed in Texas during the 1930s. He was eighty-six at that time but his memories of the slave-trading yards were undimmed by the passing years. Women were lined up in one row, men in another. A prospective buyer would walk between the rows and "grab a woman and try to throw her down and feel her to see how she's put up." If she was strong enough he would ask, "Is she a good breeder?" The buyer would then purchase a strong, black youngster of about the same age and would instruct his new acquisitions as follows: "I want you two to stay together. I want young niggers."[7]

By law, in all cases, the progeny of slave unions were the property of the slave owners as were the offspring of lower animals. "Suppose a brood mare is hired for five years, the foals belong to him who has part of the use of the dam," a nineteenth-century judge observed. He held that the "slave in Maryland in this respect, is placed on no higher or different grounds."[8]

Rewards were given to unusually procreative slave women. Some in Virginia were promised freedom after they bore a specified number of children. Apparently, there were many cases of extraordinarily fruitful slaves.[9]

Despite special privileges bestowed during pregnancy and just after childbirth, there were slave women who refused to breed children into bondage to add to the slavemaster's wealth.[10] A male slave such as Henry Bibb understood all too well that slave fathers did not fulfill the traditional paternal roles of provider and protector. He deeply regretted that he had fathered even one slave child. "She was the first and shall be the last slave that ever I will father for chains and slavery on this earth."[11] Others too were tormented by the realization that they had sired children who would be compelled to endure the degradation and misery of chattel slavery. In her moving slave narrative, Harriet (Brent) Jacobs described her ambivalent feelings toward her own infant son: "I could never forget that he was a slave. Sometimes I wished that he might die in infancy. . . . Death is better than slavery."[12] It is impossible to know the degree to which contraceptive techniques were employed by bondsmen in the antebellum period, but it is known that birth prevention was practiced in tribal Africa.[13] In addition, contraceptives and abortifacients form a fascinating part of black American folklore.[14]

Black sexual autonomy was tampered with in other ways. In the colonial period castration was not an uncommon form of punishment for unruly blacks. Such barbarism was ordinarily the work of enraged sadistic mobs as a concomitant of lynching in the post-Civil War era, but in the eighteenth century the practice was sanctioned by specific statutes. It is very significant that in all the colonies except Pennsylvania castration as a lawful punishment was reserved for Negroes and Indians. South Carolina law (1722) mandated castration for slaves who had run away for the fourth time. Emasculation was also used to punish a broad range of sexual offenses, for whites at the time were preoccupied with fears of sexual aggression by blacks. Attempted rape of a white female was the sole offense for which castration was the punishment prescribed by two Middle Atlantic states. Historian Winthrop Jordan has written that such statutes "illustrated dramatically the ease with which white men slipped over into treating their Negroes like their bulls and stallions whose 'spirit' could be subdued by emasculation.''[15]

Years after the colonies severed their bonds with Britain, this primitive practice was not unheard of. Early in the national period there was the case of the ''dangerous negro fellow'' who had attempted to deflower white women living nearby. He had expressed a strong sexual preference for Caucasian females which outraged his owner. The latter resolved to have the lecherous black gelded ''to cure him of this cursed propensity.'' The doctor who did the cutting was later informed that his patient had become a ''cool orderly slave.'' To hear the doctor tell it the black was grateful, and subsequently when the two came face to face the neutered black supposedly said, ''Tank ye, massa doctor, you did a me much great good; white or blackee women, I care not for.'' This tale was related to an English traveler in the United States by the physician himself.[16] It is entirely possible that the slave would have offered a different version.

In 1827 a convicted black rapist was sentenced by a Georgia court to be castrated and deported. The degree of white civilization in that era may be gauged by the editorial published in a local newspaper faulting the court for its softness in meting out that ''lenient'' punishment.[17]

Tenuous as the links between slave breeding and birth control may be and farfetched as the comparison between punitive castration and family planning may be in white eyes, the sexual exploitation of Americans of African descent may appear to black ''militants'' to be a seamless web, an unbroken tradition.

Undergirding that tradition is a racial mythology with strong sexual components, a mythology which has become deeply ingrained in Western civilization. On both sides of the Atlantic Englishmen thought of Africans as an inferior order of beings. Many believed them to be a separate species. Some thought them more akin to the great apes than to Homo sapiens. White opinion in Europe and the New World was virtually unanimous about the untamed, animal-like sexuality of blacks. By the late eighteenth century the idea that the African male possessed a significantly larger penis than his Caucasian counterpart was already current in Britain. A pamphlet printed there in 1772 revealed that lower class white women desired black men for reasons too brutal to explain. No explanation was necessary. An idea simultaneously so titillating and so threatening was inevitably transported to the New World. Winthrop Jordan has quoted from the journal of an officer in a Pennsylvania regiment who talked about naked black youngsters waiting on Virginia dinner tables and "how well they are hung."[18]

In 1775 a pioneer physical anthropologist, Johann Blumenbach, referred to the "remarkable genitory apparatus of an Aethiopian" he had in his anatomical collection. Blumenbach, court physician to the king of Great Britain, wrote that it was widely believed in his day that the sexual organ was inordinately larger in the black male. Passionate women, it was said, lusted for the embraces of the African. European men, he also noted, sought out African women.[19]

Richard F. Burton, the indefatigable Victorian explorer, ethnologist, linguist, and student of comparative sexual mores, endorsed the assertion that African men were more generously endowed by nature. In his privately printed *Arabian Nights* he wrote, "Debauched women prefer negroes on account of the size of their parts. . . . This is a characteristic of the negro race and African animals, e.g., the horse." He went on to say that "no honest Hindi Moslem would take his women-folk to Zanzibar on account of the huge attractions and enormous temptations there and thereby offered to them."[20]

This highly doubtful phallic theory has proven amazingly durable. Whether there has been a causal relationship between it and the castrating and lynching of blacks is questionable. Still it is axiomatic for many whites that blacks, male and female alike, are more vigorous, more unrestrained, more primitive in their sexual instincts. For this reason and possibly because of their supposed outsized genitalia, black men were seen as a clear and ever present danger. Black women, believed to be uninhibited in their lovemaking, were especially desirable as sexual partners. Slavery made them available. Our enormous mulatto population shows just how desirable and how available they were. Afro-Americans who are genetically part-white are a reminder of white male assaults on the sexuality of black females. Slave women were not raping white men. And black men ravishing white women did not produce our racially mixed population. Even the most irrational white racist will concede that much.

There are other elements in the tradition of sexual exploitation of blacks which should not be ignored if the genocide theory is to be understood. Around the turn of this century there were documented cases of black and white convicts who were sterilized. This occurred in state prisons in Indiana and elsewhere, and was motivated by the belief that surgical sterilization would suppress the sex drive and would transform disorderly prisoners into docile ones.

Only the fittest among us deserved to survive, social Darwinists preached in the dog eat dog world of early industrial America. The least fit were not entitled to procreate. Consistent with this philosophy, forty-eight boys in the Kansas Feeble Minded Institution were castrated in and around the year 1898. The following year Harry C. Sharp, a physician at the Indiana Reformatory, began to perform vasectomies. In the next nine years he credited himself with two hundred and thirty-six operations, without deleterious effects on his patients, he boasted. On the contrary, Sharp's patients developed sunnier dispositions and brighter intellects. Almost to the man they reported after the surgery that they slept better. Their appetites improved and, furthermore, they stopped their excessive masturbation.

Allowing all classes to propagate at will had had catastrophic effects on society, Sharp wrote in a medical journal in 1909. He cited the expense of supporting inmates in state institutions for the insane and mentally retarded, orphan homes, jails, workhouses, and penal institutions. With defective persons continuing to procreate freely, race degeneration, not race suicide, was the source of Sharp's anxiety. His sterilization program was a partial remedy. Sharp admitted that his patients initially resented being operated on but he said that they approved afterwards. When Sharp presented his views at a meeting of the American Medical Association in Atlantic City, there was sharp disagreement about the legal and moral justification for sterilizing prisoners. An Indianapolis physician stated flatly that moral defectives had no right to "impose another defective on the human family." Capital punishment was meted out to murderers. Depriving malefactors of the right to procreate was much less draconian a punishment, he reasoned. But another discussant, anticipating by more than six decades the dispute which is now raging about the ethics of medical experimentation behind bars, countered that prisoners as such were under duress and could not freely consent to surrender their power to reproduce.[21]

The passion to render the unfit unable to beget children was stoked partly by the concern that they were a drain on the public coffers. A Chicago jurist concurred with Professor Irving Fisher who recognized the economic benefits to society of eugenics: "our burden of taxes can be reduced by reducing the number of degenerates, delinquents and defectives supported in public institutions."[22] That was in 1922. Five years later the United States Supreme Court put its imprimatur on Virginia's sterilization act. In the case of *Buck* v. *Bell*, Justice Oliver Wendell Holmes, speaking for the majority of the tribunal, opined: "It is better for all the world, if instead of waiting to execute degenerate offspring for crime, or to let them starve for their imbecility, society can prevent those who are manifestly unfit from continuing their kind. The principle that sustains compulsory vaccination is broad enough to cover cutting the Fallopian tubes." Then, in a dictum destined to be much cited and often quoted, the venerable Justice Holmes said: "Three generations of imbeciles are enough."[23]

Racism was a frequent, almost a constant, companion of eugenics. Both seemed to reach the apex of their popularity in the first thirty or thirty-five years of this century. Disproportionately represented in the populations of public institutions, persons of African extraction were prime candidates for involuntary sterilization. Blacks were found to be intellectually wanting not because of cultural deprivation but for genetic reasons. Popenoe and Johnson, the co-authors of a standard textbook on applied eugenics, declared: "in comparison with some other races the Negro race is germinally lacking in the higher developments of intelligence."[24] Blacks were inherently predisposed to anti-social behavior, it was assumed. Popenoe, editor of the *Journal of Heredity*, and Johnson, a professor at Pittsburgh University, subscribed to the proposition of another researcher that the black American had powerful, fluctuating emotions, an improvident character, and an inclination to immoral conduct.[25] These defects were inborn rather than acquired, according to the wisdom of the day. The white race lost and the black race profited from interracial breeding, Popenoe and Johnson dogmatically asserted. They unreservedly denounced miscegenation and wanted to outlaw sexual intercourse across racial lines.[26] Extraordinarily strong development of the "procreative impulse" was thought to be a typical characteristic of the African race.[27] White blood lines could be easily defiled.

David M. Kennedy has argued in his *Birth Control in America* that in the 1920s "eugenics dominated birth control propaganda." For a time eugenicists and nativists hostile to the immigrants then flooding the United States lent their support to the birth control movement. Eager for supporters, Margaret Sanger, whose own father was an Irish immigrant, catered to xenophobic and race-purifying elements by making derogatory comments about the personal qualities of aliens. Temporarily, at least, she earned the gratitude of many a bigot by announcing that she wanted the fit to have more children and the unfit to produce fewer children. Subsequently, Mrs. Sanger, made somewhat uneasy by the racists and know-nothings who had embraced her, refined her definition of the "unfit." She meant the physically deformed and feebleminded, she explained, not particular races or religions. After realizing that voluntary birth control would not advance their elitist policies, the majority of eugenicists turned against Margaret Sanger. Nevertheless, her flirtation with eugenics and nativism remains a blot on her movement's otherwise excellent record.

In 1929 Dr. Thurman B. Rice, who taught at the Indiana

University School of Medicine, published a book euphemistically titled *Racial Hygiene*, in which he advocated castration as the suitable punishment and preventive technique for sex criminals. For other categories of unfit persons, for the feebleminded, for epileptics, for the insane, and deformed, he recommended vasectomies. These remedies were not prescribed only for blacks but the author did not hesitate to express his trepidation as he contemplated racial mongrelization, the curse of South America. "The colored races are pressing the white race most urgently," Rice wrote "and this pressure may be expected to increase."[28]

Sterilizations involving both sexes were performed during the 1930s and 1940s at the State Hospital for Negroes located in Goldsboro, North Carolina. The percentage of black males sterilized there was higher than the percentage in comparable white institutions in North Carolina. Black rapists and blacks who were troublesome to hospital authorities were castrated to tranquilize them and make them more manageable. Consent to be sterilized was not sought from the patients in advance of the operations, supposedly because of their low intelligence, but it is alleged that they raised no objections. Relatives were asked for permission, but procedural safeguards appear to have been inadequate.[29] Black sexuality was something of a plaything.

Disclosure of a forty-year-old U.S. Public Health Service research project involving syphilitic black men is another stark reminder of the subhuman status to which blacks have been consigned.[30] The so-called Tuskegee study began in the autumn of 1932 in the midst of the Great Depression. It was concentrated in rural Macon County in eastern Alabama. Approximately six hundred males, all black, poor, and uneducated, were recruited for the research, the main purpose of which was to allow investigators to observe the effects of untreated syphilis over a prolonged period of time. The subjects were divided into three subgroups. Individuals who had been under medical care for syphilis during the first two years of infection were placed in one group. A second group consisted of men suffering from syphilis who had never received any treatment for their disease. Into the third group were placed healthy persons who had never manifested any symptoms of the dread venereal disease.

Diverse means were employed to insure the cooperation of subjects over the years. Some of these imaginative techniques were listed in an article written in 1953 by a public health nurse, a venereal disease field investigator, and two physicians associated with the study. Medicines had been provided free of charge as was burial insurance. On those days when followup physical examinations were scheduled there were free hot meals. Being chauffered to and from the hospital in a new government-owned station wagon was still another perquisite.[31]

The human subjects were never apprised of the nature of the project or told why they had been recruited as participants. None was ever informed that he had syphilis. Charles Pollard, one of the human guinea pigs involved in the project, survived to testify that he and the others were merely informed that they had "bad blood."[32] Subjects were not given medical attention for their illness and allegedly were discouraged or prevented from obtaining treatment from other sources.[33] In March 1973 the Senate Subcommittee on Health chaired by Senator Edward Kennedy was told by Fred Gray, an attorney for some forty of the still living participants in the Tuskegee study, that a program had been launched in Macon County in the late 1940s and early 1950s to have all syphilitics treated. However, the Tuskegee sample was not allowed to benefit.[34] Since 1932 a number of blacks whose syphilitic condition went untreated have died. How many of their deaths were actually caused or hastened by their failure to receive proper medication we shall never know. Presumably, penicillin and the "miracle"-working antibiotics could have saved many who were, in effect, condemned to death.

The racial element in the Tuskegee project is crucial. Fred Gray told Senator Kennedy that the experimentation was racially motivated. Not a single white subject had been selected for the study.[35] There were whites afflicted with the disease who were living in Macon County in 1932. Why were they not invited to join the experimental sample? Why were only blacks solicited? It has been alleged in court that "the black subjects were selected and used in the experiment . . . solely because of their race and color in violation of their rights secured by the Constitution and Laws of the United States." In a billion dollar lawsuit* filed on behalf of the surviving participants and for the heirs or estates of deceased subjects, lawyers for the plaintiffs described the Tuskegee medical study as a "program of controlled genocide."

For serving as guinea pigs for four decades Charles Pollard, a poor farmer in his late sixties, and the other living Tuskegee subjects have received a paltry twenty-five dollars each. Black members of the United States House of Representatives have demanded reparations for the surviving victims and have asked that those responsible for the Nazi-like study be brought to justice.[36] Of course, no monetary settlement can adequately compensate Pollard, the other victims, and their heirs for the monstrous wrong done them in the name of medical science. Still, a legal victory in the suit brought on their behalf by the NAACP Legal Defense and Educational Fund would be a partial atonement for this officially sanctioned crime. Defendants named in the litigation are the United States of America, which is held to be ultimately responsible; the Department of Health, Education and Welfare and its Secretary, Caspar Weinberger; the U.S. Public Health Service; the U.S. Center for Disease Control, Venereal Disease Branch; the State of Alabama; the Milbank Memorial Fund which provided funds for pathological examinations; and others.

Nazi physicians, many of them pillars of the German medical establishment, were found guilty by a Nuremberg tribunal for

---

*Terms of an out-of-court settlement of the suit were officially announced in February, 1975. Survivors who had been afflicted with syphilis were to be awarded $37,500 each by the federal government. To the estate of every deceased syphilitic participant $15,000 was to be paid. The same amount was due each living participant in the project who did not have syphilis. The federal government also agreed to pay $5,000 to the estate of each deceased participant who had not had syphilis.

performing brutal experiments on concentration camp prisoners. But criminal action against those persons responsible for planning and carrying out the Tuskegee project is inconceivable. Why? Like the uncivilized Nazi experimentation, the syphilis investigations were quite legal. Both were conducted under the auspices of lawfully constituted governments. Obviously, death camp inmates did not volunteer to be guinea pigs. In a real sense neither did the poor, hapless blacks in rural Alabama. Deprived of sufficient knowledge of their illness and not understanding the character and purpose of the study, they could not make the decision that is required to meet the ethical standards set forth at Nuremberg for medical experimentation.

Almost forty years elapsed before the startling public revelation of the syphilis study. During that time, however, the research was anything but a carefully guarded secret. Progress reports were periodically published in medical and public health journals, a fact which makes the entire episode all the more disturbing.

Widely and feelingly discussed in black communities, the project has occasionally been misrepresented. For example, social critic-humorist Dick Gregory, has stated publicly that the black subjects had been injected with syphilis and that Tuskegee was the site chosen for the study because it is the home of Booker T. Washington's famous educational institute. Black students from all over the country gravitated there and were part of the sample, Gregory implied. He further intimated that the project organizers wanted black students to return to their respective communities to spread the crippling and death-dealing disease.[37] There was no need for Gregory to embellish and distort the facts. The unembellished truth is horrible enough.

## NOTES

1. Office of Planning and Research, U.S. Department of Labor, *The Case for National Action—Negro Family* (March 1965). The report argued that the black family in the urban ghetto was crumbling. What was

required was a national effort directed to a new kind of national goal: the establishment of a stable Negro family structure.

2. Frederick Bancroft, *Slave-Trading in the Old South* (Baltimore: J. H. Furst Co., 1931), p. 81.

3. Robert William Fogel and Stanley L. Engerman, *Time on the Cross—The Economics of American Negro Slavery* (Boston: Little, Brown and Co., 1974), pp. 78-86.

4. Frederick Douglass, *Life and Times of Frederick Douglass* (Hartford: Park Publishing Co., 1882), pp. 118-119.

5. Quoted in George P. Rawick, *From Sundown to Sunup—The Making of the Black Community* (Westport, Conn.: Greenwood Publishing Co., 1972), p. 88. These interviews were conducted as part of the Slave Narrative Collection of the Federal Writers Project of the Works Project Administration in the 1930s.

6. James Roberts, *The Narrative of James Roberts* (Chicago: Printed for the Author, 1858), p. 26.

7. Norman R. Yetman (ed.), *Life Under the "Peculiar Institution"—Selections from the Slave Narrative Collection* (New York: Holt, Rinehart and Winston Inc., 1970), p. 288.

8. William Goodell, *The American Slave Code in Theory and Practice* (New York: The New American Library, 1969), p. 30. This book was originally published in 1853.

9. There was a pattern of natural growth of the slave population in the United States discernible by the eighteenth century. See Philip D. Curtin, *The Atlantic Slave Trade—A Census* (Madison: The University of Wisconsin Press, 1969), pp. 28-29, 73, 92. In the Caribbean, however, there appears to have been a marked decrease of the slave population. Tannenbaum has written that to the great consternation of slave masters in the West Indies, slave women frequently did not have children. Induced and spontaneous abortions were common. See Frank Tannenbaum, *Slave and Citizen: The Negro in the Americas* (New York: Vintage Books, 1946), pp. 38-39.

10. Margaret Jane Blake, *Memoirs of Margaret Jane Blake of Baltimore, Maryland* (Philadelphia: Press of Innes and Son, 1897), p. 13.

11. Henry Bibb, *Narrative of the Life and Times of Henry Bibb, An American Slave* (New York: Published by the Author, 1850), p. 44.

12. Harriet (Brent) Jacobs, *Incidents in the Life of a Slave Girl*, ed. L. Maria Child (Boston: Published for the Author, 1861), p. 96. Also see

Anonymous and Thomas H. Jones, *The Experience of Thomas H. Jones Who Was a Slave for Forty-Three Years* (New Bedford: E. Anthony and Sons, 1871), p. 8.

13. Norman E. Himes, *Medical History of Contraception* (Baltimore: The Williams and Wilkins Co., 1936), pp. 5-12.

14. Newbell Niles Puckett, *Folk Beliefs of the Southern Negro* (New York: Negro Universities Press, 1968), pp. 331-332.

15. Winthrop D. Jordan, *White Over Black—American Attitudes Toward the Negro 1550-1812* (Chapel Hill: University of North Carolina Press, 1968), pp. 154-159.

16. Charles William Janson, *The Stranger in America, 1793-1806* (New York: The Press of the Pioneers Inc., 1935), pp. 386-387.

17. Ralph Betts Flanders, *Plantation Slavery in Georgia* (Cos Cob, Conn.: John E. Edwards, Publisher, 1967), p. 267.

18. Winthrop D. Jordan, *The White Man's Burden—Historical Origins of Racism in the United States* (London: Oxford University Press, 1974), p. 83.

19. Johann Friedrich Blumenbach, *The Anthropological Treatises of Johann Friedrich Blumenbach*, trans. Thomas Blendyshe (London: Longman, Green, Longman, Roberts & Green, 1865), p. 249.

20. Richard F. Burton (trans.) *The Book of the Thousand Nights and A Night—A Plain and Literal Translation of the Arabian Nights Entertainment* (n.p., Privately Printed by the Burton Club, n.d.), I, 6.

21. Harry C. Sharp, *The Sterilization of Degenerates*, Reprint of a paper read before the American Prison Association at Chicago, 1909. Also see Harry C. Sharp, "Vasectomy as a Means of Preventing Procreation in Defectives," *Journal of the American Medical Association* 53, No. 23 (1909): 1897-1902.

22. See Harry Olson's Introduction to Harry Hamilton Laughlin, *Eugenical Sterilization in the United States* (Chicago: Psychopathic Laboratory of the Municipal Court of Chicago, 1922), p. v.

23. 274 U.S. 200 (1927).

24. Paul Popenoe and Roswell Hill Johnson, *Applied Eugenics* (New York: The Macmillan Co., 1918), p. 284.

25. Ibid., p. 290.

26. Ibid., pp. 292, 296.

27. John Moffatt Mecklin, *Democracy and Race Friction* (New York: The Macmillan Co., 1914), p. 58.

28. Thurman B. Rice, *Racial Hygiene—A Practical Discussion of*

*Eugenics and Race Culture* (New York: The Macmillan Co., 1929), pp. 318-320, 368.

29. Moya Woodside, *Sterilization in North Carolina: A Sociological and Psychological Study* (Chapel Hill: The University of North Carolina Press, 1950), pp. 31-33.

30. *New York Times*, 26, 27, 28 July 1972.

31. Eunice Rivers, R.N., Stanley H. Shuman, M.D., Lloyd Simpson, and Sidney Olansky, M.D., "Twenty Years of Followup Experience in a Long-Range Medical Study," *Public Health Reports* 68, No. 4 (April 1953): 391-392.

32. *Hearings Before the Subcommittee on Health of the Committee on Labor and Public Welfare—United States Senate—Ninety-Third Congress—First Session On S. 974,* 7 and 8 March 1973, Part 3 (Washington, D.C.: U.S. Government Printing Office, 1973), p. 1036.

33. Complaint in *Charles W. Pollard et al.* v. *the United States of America et al.*, Civil Action No. 4126-N in the United States District Court, Middle District of Alabama Northern Division.

34. *Hearings*, p. 1034.

35. Ibid., p. 1035.

36. *Jet*, 17 August 1972.

37. Gregory made these remarks as a panel discussant at the University of Rhode Island, Kingston, R. I., on 6 April 1974.

# 4. *The Black Debate Begins—Quality vs. Quantity*

Scholars have paid scant attention to the genocide rhetoric as it relates to the touchy topics of contraception, abortion, and sterilization. Very little has been written about the sources of the genocide-birth control ideological nexus which are the major foci of this book. Why should birth control have become linked to a theory of genocide?

What may well be the taproot of the link is the conviction, as old as history itself, that in numbers there is strength. That conviction began to emerge when black Americans began to argue the merits of birth control and population control shortly after Margaret Sanger founded her first clinic in Brownsville. Before long the debate became pivotal. From the beginning, black opinion varied greatly. Eugenics, theology, public health, and demography all entered in.

Kelly Miller, an esteemed essayist and one of America's leading black thinkers for more than forty years until his death in 1939, was troubled by the extremely low birth rate of highly educated blacks, a demographic phenomenon that has remained unchanged ever since. At Howard University where Miller was dean of the

College of Arts and Sciences, the black faculty was not even producing enough issue to replace themselves in the overall black population. Upper-class Afro-Americans, the intellectual elite, were heading toward extinction, Professor Miller feared. They were deliberately shirking the responsibility of parenthood because they did not wish to bring children into a society that held blacks in contempt. On the other hand, the black masses which, in the future, would have to replenish the supply of black professionals were multiplying and making merry.[1]

Upset by the unplanned reproduction of the black poor, Dr. W. E. B. DuBois became one of the first blacks to put his seal of approval on family planning. DuBois, one of the giants of the black liberation struggle, was born in Great Barrington, Massachusetts, in 1868 and died in Accra, Ghana, in 1963. Profoundly disappointed by the snail's pace at which the civil rights movement was progressing, he abandoned the United States in his twilight years and became a Ghanaian citizen. DuBois lived a full if frustrating life. A brilliant student, he was educated at Fisk University and the University of Berlin and earned a Ph.D. from Harvard. His considerable scholarly attainments included historical treatises on the *Suppression of the African Slave Trade* and *Black Reconstruction* and an incisive sociological study of the *Philadelphia Negro.* But the unflagging efforts of this black titan as a crusader for racial justice at least equaled his academic achievements. In pursuit of that goal he relentlessly assailed the ears of his countrymen for more than half a century. He labored tirelessly against lynching and the indignities of Jim Crowism. Starting in the 1890s he offered black Americans a meaningful alternative to the submissive philosophy of Booker T. Washington. To DuBois, Booker T. practically accepted the alleged inferiority of the Negro and his second-class citizenship status. DuBois was instrumental in creating the NAACP in 1910 and for two decades served as editor of its monthly magazine, *The Crisis.* Cold and arrogant in the opinion of some who dealt with him, DuBois was nonetheless deeply committed to uplifting the downtrodden black man in Africa and the Caribbean as well as in the United States.

More than half a century ago DuBois, writing in *The Crisis*, gave a ringing endorsement to birth control, calling it "science and sense applied to the bringing of children into the world." Of all who required it, Dr. DuBois added, "we Negroes are first." Having endless children resulted in a criminally high infant mortality rate and it was inimical to the health of women. A second alternative, postponing marriage until middle age lest unwanted children be brought into the world, DuBois rejected. Family planning was clearly preferable and would redound to the well-being of both parents and offspring.[2]

Ten years later DuBois lamented the fact that grass-roots black opinion was totally ignorant of birth control. Other blacks, educated ones included, regarded it as inherently immoral.[3] To those blacks who took a jaundiced view of birth control, religious and moral considerations probably counted for more than demographic factors. In 1934 the seventh annual convention of Marcus Garvey's Universal Negro Improvement Association met in Kingston, Jamaica. The Garveyites, black nationalists par excellence, unanimously passed a resolution condemning birth control. Curiously, the resolution read much like a papal encyclical. Moved by an American black and seconded by a West Indian delegate, the resolution averred that "any attempt to interfere with the natural function of life is a rebellion against the conceived purpose of divinity in making man a part of his spiritual self." The convention counseled persons of African descent throughout the world not to "accept or practice the theory of birth control such as is being advocated by irresponsible speculators who are attempting to interfere with the course of nature and with the purpose of the God in whom we believe."[4]

A Nashville, Tennessee, study in 1940, using a sample of southern urban black mothers, concluded that about 50 percent regarded birth control practices unfavorably. The sinfulness of contraception was the most prevalent reason cited. Other major explanations offered were the inefficiency of birth control and the feeling that it was harmful to the practitioner's health.[5]

In a study carried out nine years later in Nashville, approximately one-third of the subjects reacted negatively to birth control. Half of these offered religious objections. "The Lord put us on earth to multiply," one subject commented in an interview. "And I trust the Lord. He made me and when I have had all I'm supposed to have, then I'll quit. Can't have any more than the Lord says. And to use them birth controls would mean I'm messin' with the Lord's business."[6] Disapproval by husbands also accounted for some negative female attitudes toward birth control. Not uncommonly, black men had superstitious phobias about impotence which they feared could result from interfering with a natural process.[7]

During the Great Depression, which caused incalculable suffering among black Americans, educated blacks who wrote on family planning favored it as a necessary and desirable part of good health care. The June 1932 issue of the *Birth Control Review* focused on the underprivileged blacks' great need for planned parenthood, on the deficiency of family planning services, and on Negro receptivity to birth control.

Elmer Carter, editor of *Opportunity,* pointed out that since the economic collapse, myriad lower-class black women had sought out unqualified quack abortionists to terminate unwanted pregnancies. The real question then was whether birth control would be achieved by safe contraceptive means or by "the clumsy almost murderous methods of the medical racketeer." At that juncture the leading black communities on Chicago's South Side and in Harlem were served by only two birth control clinics. Carter wrote that it would be most unfortunate if the birth control movement remained "unmindful or indifferent to the plight of the Negro."[8] Dr. Charles H. Garvin, a prominent black surgeon practicing in Cleveland, also indicated that the movement had been dilatory in its work among blacks.[9]

Contraception had made significant inroads in the educated black classes. And when birth control clinics were established in Baltimore, Detroit, and Cincinnati, the blacks attended out of proportion to their share of the population of those cities. By the mid-1930s blacks in Harlem already had rather low birth rates. Several explanations were possible, but, in the judgment of one demographer, it seemed likely that the fertility situation reflected a "deliberate limitation of families among married couples who can ill afford more children in the city."[10] Pregnancy-spacing facilities were also made available to blacks in Berkely County, a rural county in South Carolina with a tenant farmer population. No less than 80 percent of the contacted black persons with low incomes and little schooling utilized the child-spacing methods put at their disposal.[11]

However, child-spacing methods were rarely available. Poor women, including of course the overwhelming majority of black women, were conscripted to child-bearing. They had no real option in the matter. All avenues of contraceptive information were blocked, Margaret Sanger wrote in *The Crisis* in 1934. Women were expected to bring forth babies regardless of the effect on their own health or the well-being of their children, regardless of their husbands' ability to feed additional mouths. The consequence was "wasted lives of women—tortured and broken in child-bearing. Twelve children born—three alive—or twenty pregnancies, with five children to show for the waste. It's barbarous, it's inhuman, it's a waste of woman power and child life." Women, Mrs. Sanger asserted, were enslaved as the black race had never been enslaved. Where was their great emancipator, their Abraham Lincoln? Margaret Sanger resolved to be that emancipator. Her task was to be herculean.[12]

To meet the family planning needs of Black Americans the Birth Control Federation* formed a Division of Negro Service. Its

---

*The Birth Control Federation of America was the formal organization of the Birth Control Council, a coalition of the American Birth Control League (1921), and the Clinical Research Bureau (which later became the Margaret Sanger Research Bureau). In 1941 the Birth Control Federation of America changed its name to the Planned Parenthood Federation of America, Inc. Since 1963 to signify its merger with the World Population Emergency Campaign and to indicate its interest in family

national advisory council on Negro problems included Dr.
DuBois; Mary McLeod Bethune, founder and head of the National
Council of Negro Women; Walter White, executive director of the
NAACP; Reverend Adam Clayton Powell, Jr., pastor of the
Abyssinian Baptist Church; Professor E. Franklin Frazier; and
other prominent blacks. The council supplied public speakers on
family planning to interested groups of which there were many.
Printed literature and materials for exhibit were other conduits for
conveying the birth control message.

During World War II the advisory council made an appeal for
action on planned parenthood. In the face of problems of grinding
poverty and disease which bedeviled blacks, in the light of their
distressingly high infant and maternal mortality rates, it was stated
that the planning of parenthood was not merely desirable but was
essential to further strengthening the nation's health and welfare.

Among the approximately thirteen million black Americans, the
death rate was 50 percent greater than among Americans of
European background. Black life expectancy was twelve years
less. Black babies perished at a rate one and a half times that of
whites and black mothers died at twice the rate of whites. These
cold statistics reflected what the Division of Negro Service aptly
called "a national health deficit" and represented "a social loss
. . . in marred, broken and unproductive lives."[13] Child-spacing
information and services were not a cure-all for the myriad ills of
black Americans, but they were recognized by black birth controllers as an important step forward.

The advisory council called upon state public health services to
make planned parenthood an integral part of their health programs.
Private organizations on the federal, state, and local levels were
implored to educate parents about "planned, rather than
haphazard, preparation for parenthood." While the appeal was
made in the interests of the entire populace, there was an explicit

planning programs throughout the world, the organization has used the
name Planned Parenthood-World Population.

statement that in this area of health protection the disproportionately greater need of black citizens had to be met without further delay.

Members of the medical profession, black and white, were specifically urged to make extra efforts to impart knowledge of family planning to all Americans who needed and wanted it. Persons of African descent had been excluded from the American Medical Association in seventeen southern states and Washington, D.C. This had led in 1895 to the founding of the black National Medical Association. Boasting a membership of three thousand Afro-American physicians in 1943, the NMA was in the vanguard of the family planning movement among blacks. Sessions in pregnancy spacing were held at its national conventions and, beginning in January 1941, its administrative structure included a subcommittee on planned parenthood. Family planning was frequently a topic of articles and reports in its official publication.[14]

Also spearheading the black birth control crusade was the National Council of Negro Women. It had been born in 1935 through the efforts of Mary McLeod Bethune, a remarkably able woman. Her protracted friendship with the First Lady, Eleanor Roosevelt, enhanced her considerable influence. "No other black woman before or since has enjoyed so much concentration of power in a single individual," wrote the author of a 1973 article on women in politics.[15] At its annual meeting in 1941 the National Council of Negro Women passed a resolution asking the health committee of every black organization not to neglect family planning programs which aimed "to aid each family to have all the children it can afford and support but no more—in order to insure better health, security and happiness for all." To make certain that the resolution was implemented, the council, an umbrella organization for fourteen major black women's groups, created a standing committee on family planning. Progress reports were periodically published in its official voice, the *Afroamerican Women's Journal.*[16]

A. Philip Randolph lent his prestige to the fledgling black birth control movement. As creator and international president of the Brotherhood of Sleeping Car Porters, Randolph may rightly be described as the most important and powerful trade unionist in black American history. Today Randolph is recognized as the elder statesman of the civil rights movement. It is difficult to believe that at one time in American history, owing to Randolph's socialism and his opposition to black American participation in World War I, the FBI considered him to be the most dangerous black man in the country. A promotional flyer distributed by the Planned Parenthood Federation quoted Randolph as follows: "Better schools, better employment, better medical and recreational facilities will do much to produce a better generation, but planning for health must begin at home and if possible even before the next generation is born. Family planning is the first step in attaining this goal."[17]

Despite the foregoing, family planning remained a delicate topic. Even some middle-class black institutions were chary about giving their unqualified support to the movement. In March 1947 the *Pittsburgh Courier,* one of the most influential Negro weeklies, published an article entitled "Planned Parenthood Has the Answers to Questions Concerning Health and Happiness of the Family."[18] A few weeks later a letter to the editor from a Roman Catholic priest who had worked among black people criticized the *Courier* for advocating a practice that was not only a violation of God's law but one which would decimate the black race.[19] The newspaper retorted defensively that the article in question was actually a news release from a planned parenthood agency. The *Courier* did not necessarily endorse the philosophy of family planning.

The argument that birth control was a vehicle by which blacks would be decimated or by which they would decimate themselves was not novel in the 1940s. Marcus Garvey, who is regarded by many black separatists today as the progenitor of the black power phenomenon, seems to have said little about birth control per se but he was concerned about the tragedy of racial extinction. He wanted his Universal Negro Improvement Association (UNIA) to strengthen the black race so as to eliminate the possibility that blacks could be exterminated, as he contended the American Indian had been. In his *Philosophy and Opinions*, first published in 1923, the Jamaican-born black nationalist cautioned blacks against supinely permitting "the great white race to lift itself in numbers and power." In another five centuries that would mean that this "full grown race of white men will in turn exterminate the weaker race of black men for the purpose of finding enough room on this limited mundane sphere to accommodate that race which will have numerically multiplied itself into many billions."[20] Global black solidarity was imperative, Garvey declared, but he did not tell blacks to multiply pell mell or admonish them to forsake contraception.

Garvey was probably the premier black nationalist in American history. He had first set foot in the United States in March 1916. Born twenty nine years earlier in St. Ann's Bay, Jamaica, in the British West Indies, Garvey was a stocky, ebony-skinned man. No fanfare attended his arrival in 1916, but for the next eleven years he was to claim infinitely more than his share of the limelight. His success in building what one historian has called "the first and only really mass movement among Negroes" was attributable to many factors. Among these were his showmanship, his flair for public relations, and the pageantry he offered the poor black community. Garbed in a military uniform or an academic gown, Garvey himself was the center of attraction at his mammoth rallies and colorful parades which injected pride and excitement into the otherwise drab lives of the ghetto masses. He possessed that extremely rare combination of qualities that is today called charisma.

Garvey also purveyed a black nationalist philosophy designed to invigorate the sagging self-esteem of black Americans. The times were propitious for black nationalism. Fellow immigrants from the Caribbean sought a spokesman for their interests and for their aspirations which had been stifled by a racist, segregated society.

Black southern agricultural workers who had migrated to northern urban areas seeking economic opportunity and racial equality were bitterly disappointed with city life above the Mason-Dixon line. World War I and its turbulent aftermath, the era of Garvey's greatest popularity, was also a period of almost unparalleled interracial strife and black unrest. Lynching and race rioting continued unabated during the Great War. So bloody was the summer of 1919 that it was dubbed the "Red Summer." Against this background of carnage and amid the ensuing climate of disillusionment and hopelessness, Garvey was able to attract followers by the hundreds of thousands, perhaps by the millions.

Eloquently preaching race pride, this magnetic evangelist of black nationalism fully exploited his opportunity. Directing his appeal to the darker complected Negroes in particular, Garvey rhapsodized about blacks and blackness. He eulogized the glorious past of the Africans and prophesied an equally glorious future. Black skin was not a badge of inferiority. On the contrary, Garvey taught that it represented beauty and power. In many respects the cocky Jamaican planted the seeds of the "black is beautiful" philosophy which germinated in the black revolution of the 1960s. Garvey, of course, did not live to see that happen. In February 1925 he was imprisoned, having been convicted of fraudulently using the United States mails to raise funds for his major commercial enterprise, the Black Star Steamship Line. After serving two years and nine months of his term, President Calvin Coolidge commuted the rest of his sentence. He was released from the Atlanta federal penitentiary and swiftly deported to his birthplace as an undesirable alien. He died in relative obscurity in London in 1940.

Black nationalists like Garvey were not alone in their desire to see the continued growth of the black population in America. Negro anthropologist W. Montague Cobb, writing in 1939, expected life in the United States to become increasingly competitive because the American population would be growing within fixed territorial limits. He speculated about the chances of the white majority liquidating the competing black minority. His prescription for the Afro-American was as follows:

He should maintain his high birthrate observing the conditions of life necessary to this end. This alone has made him able to increase in spite of decimating mortality hardships. If the tide should turn against him later, strength will be better than weakness in numbers.[21]

DuBois had written almost impatiently about those who are "led away by the fallacy of numbers. They want the black race to survive. They are cheered by a census return of increasing numbers and a high rate of increase." To DuBois the numbers game was deplorable. He believed that fellow blacks had to learn that "among human races and groups, as among vegetables, quality and not mere quantity really counts."[22]

Higher fertility among blacks in the depths of the depression would not mean a population gain because poverty, malnutrition, and disease were raising the death rate. Why enrich the undertakers and pack the prisons with unwanted children, asked George Schuyler. "It were far better to have less children and improve the social and physical well-being of those they have."[23] Beginning in 1926 Schuyler had served as a columnist and editorial writer for the *Pittsburgh Courier,* perhaps the most widely read black weekly in the depression-ridden 1930s. In more recent years Schuyler turned sharply to the right and has even been called a black John Bircher.

Another writer noted in Malthusian terms that the size of the black population was restricted not by a low birth rate "but mainly by the brutal and barbarous checks of malnutrition, disease, and death."[24]

Dr. Charles Garvin also fired a verbal salvo at those who contended that dissemination of birth control information would promote "race suicide." Birth control was salutary for blacks and would lead to "race preservation and advancement." Garvin was vitally concerned with enhanced "racial stamina" which would be achieved by "fewer and stronger babies, higher quality, low quantity production."[25]

The relationship between the fertility of the black race and its salvation was again the subject of debate at the end of World War II. Arguments on both sides changed little, if at all. Taking issue with those whom he labeled the "self-appointed guardians of the Negro race," E. Franklin Frazier, the distinguished black sociologist, maintained that "more and more babies born indiscriminately, without thought of the parent's health or ability to rear them, is not the answer." Black survival and progress were not contingent upon the number of babies born but on the number who lived to become strong, healthy adults. Frazier, though a vociferous champion of planned parenthood for many years, did not view it as a panacea for the assorted ills of the American Negro. However, he insisted that "to live decently and efficiently, whether his relative numbers are greater or smaller will depend upon knowledge and the intelligent ordering of his life rather than upon ignorance and uncontrolled impulse."[26]

In 1945 one of the "self-appointed guardians" of the race was Dr. Julian Lewis, a pathologist and former professor at the University of Chicago. Whereas the growth of the white race was guaranteed by a low death rate, he wrote in the *Negro Digest,* the survival of the black race in the United States was dependent upon a high birth rate. Instead of reducing the black population Lewis wanted to resolve the multiple problems of illiteracy, deficient medical facilities, and congested living conditions which curtailed black longevity. He categorically denied that lowering the number of blacks would improve conditions in schools or hospitals, for example.[27]

Almost a decade later Lewis was still apprehensive about blacks becoming an "inconspicuous group" rather than the country's largest minority. This could happen, he declared, if the black and white birth rates were equalized and the prevailing death rate for blacks was unchanged. He faulted the Planned Parenthood Federation for trying to "improve the quality of the human race at the cost of numbers.'' If blacks practice birth control on a general scale it would mean ''race suicide,'' Lewis said.''[28]

''Race suicide'' was the fashionable phrase at that juncture in history. Before too long it was supplanted by ''genocide.'' Blacks started to use the term, particularly after the publication in 1951 of William Patterson's book, *We Charge Genocide—The Historic Petition to the United Nations for Relief from a Crime of the United States Government Against the Negro People.*

Patterson concerned himself with documenting sundry forms of genocide, including acts of terrorism, harassment by police, deplorable ghetto living conditions, disfranchisement, job discrimination, and inaccessible medical therapy. In the first edition of the book, the question of birth control was not raised. But nineteen years later, when a second edition was published, Patterson stated that, ''Measures to prevent birth within the group [American Negroes] are practiced in several states.''[29]

## NOTES

1. Kelly Miller, ''Eugenics of the Negro Race,'' *The Scientific Monthly* 5 (July 1917): 57-59.

2. W. E. B. DuBois, ''Birth,'' *The Crisis*, October 1922, pp. 248-250.

3. W. E. B. DuBois ''Black Folk and Birth Control,'' *Birth Control Review*, June 1932, pp. 166-167.

4. *The Black Man*, November 1934.

5. Preston Valien and Alberta Price Fitzgerald, ''Attitudes of the Negro Mother Toward Birth Control'' *American Journal of Sociology* 55 (1949): 279-283.

6. Preston Valien and Ruth E. Vaughn, ''Birth Control Attitudes and Practices of Negro Mothers,'' *Sociology and Social Research* 35, No. 6 (July-August 1951): 417.

7. Dorothy Boulding Ferebee, ''Planned Parenthood As a Public Health Measure for the Negro Race,'' *Human Fertility* 7, No. 1 (February 1942): 7-10; Robert E. Seibels, ''A Rural Project in Negro Maternal Health,'' *Human Fertility* 6, No. 2 (April 1941): 42-44.

8. Elmer A. Carter, "Eugenics for the Negro," *Birth Control Review*, June 1932, pp. 169-170.

9. Charles H. Garvin, "The Negro Doctor's Task," *Birth Control Review*, November 1932, pp. 269-270.

10. Clyde V. Kiser, "Fertility of Harlem Negroes," *Milbank Memorial Fund Quarterly* 13, No. 3 (July 1935): 284.

11. Seibels, "A Rural Project in Negro Maternal Health," p. 44. In the early 1930s a large study had shown that black women had practiced contraception much less widely and much less effectively than white women. See Raymond Pearl, "Fertility and Contraception in Urban Whites and Negroes," *Science* 83 (22 May 1936): 503-506.

12. Margaret Sanger, "The Case for Birth Control," *The Crisis* 41, No. 6 (June 1934): 177.

13. *Better Health for 13,000,000* (New York: Planned Parenthood Federation of America, 1943), p. 5.

14. Ibid., p. 26.

15. Ethel Payne, "Women in Politics," *Dawn Magazine*, October 1973, p. 25.

16. *Better Health*, p. 27.

17. *Planned Parenthood Means Better Families* (n.p., n.d.).

18. *Pittsburgh Courier*, 29 March 1947.

19. Ibid., 19 April 1947.

20. Marcus Garvey, *Philosophy and Opinions of Marcus Garvey*, ed. Amy Jacques Garvey (London: Frank Cass and Co. Ltd., 1967), pp. 46-48. Garvey himself was one of eleven children, only two of whom reached adulthood.

21. W. Montague Cobb, "The Negro as a Biological Element in the American Population," *Journal of Negro Education* 8 No. 3 (July 1939): 345-346.

22. DuBois, "Black Folk and Birth Control," pp. 166-167.

23. George Schuyler, "Quantity or Quality," *Birth Control Review*, June 1932, pp. 165-166.

24. Walter A. Terpenning, "God's Chillun," *Birth Control Review*, June 1932, pp. 171-172.

25. Charles H. Garvin, "The Negro Doctor's Task," *Birth Control Review,* November 1932, pp. 269-270.

26. E. Franklin Frazier, "Birth Control for More *Negro Babies*," *Negro Digest* 3 (July 1945): 41-44.

27. Julian Lewis, "Can the Negro Afford Birth Control," *Negro Digest* 3 (May 1945): 19-22.

28. "Is Birth Control a Menace? To Negroes," *Jet*, 19 August 1954, pp. 52-55.

29. William L. Patterson (ed.), *We Charge Genocide—The Historic Petition to the United Nations for Relief from a Crime of the United States Government Against the Negro People* (New York: International Publishers, 1970), p. xi.

# 5 . "Strength in Numbers" —An Old and Oft-Told Tale

The "strength in numbers" ideology has not been peculiar to black Americans. Various national, ethnic, racial, and religious groups have voiced their anxiety about the possible long-range effects of birth control.

Starting with the age of the Reformation religious passions were periodically rekindled by sectarian numerical competition. At the end of the nineteenth century a combination of largely Catholic immigration and a slump in white Anglo-Saxon fertility dismayed some Protestants in the United States. America could be swamped by hordes of hated papists. Because abortion was among the reasons for the dip in Protestant fertility, some Protestant ministers assumed strong anti-abortion positions. One New England divine in 1891, horrified by the prospect of Catholic overlordship, reproached his congregants: "We are told that the Roman Catholics are going to possess New England. Through your sin [abortion] they may do so."

On the other side Professor John T. Noonan, a distinguished Catholic scholar, has shown that a few decades ago some clerics in the mother church regarded contraception as a potential danger because it "could deprive society of a fair share of Catholics." Those prelates thought that the Church might expand if Catholics limited their reproductive activities less than other people.[1]

There were also those who were convinced that general use of contraceptives would result in the extinction of the species. The irrelevance of this "race suicide" argument to specific acts of contraception and its absurdity in the face of demographic changes has led to its virtual obsolescence, at least insofar as undifferentiated Homo sapiens are concerned.

Rabid nationalism has often spawned pro-natalism. Modern history is replete with case studies. Fascist Italy engaged in what Benito Mussolini with his penchant for martial slogans called the "battle for births." What Italy needed badly was "demographic rejuvenation." Numbers were power, he proclaimed. Celibacy was disloyal, a cardinal sin, except for cardinals and lower ranking clergy, of course. Unmarried lay men between twenty-five and sixty-five years of age were subject to a bachelor's tax.[2] Among the poor, Mussolini inaugurated a "baby marathon," a stork derby. Prizes were given to those producing three or more offspring in a three-year period. Newlyweds, their right arms extended in the fascist salute, pledged to have a dozen children for the motherland. To the carrot of patriotic inducement was added the stick of repression. Writing in favor of contraception violated a law passed in 1926. Five years hence a new penal code included a provision which forbade sterilization. A second provision made it a crime punishable by fine and imprisonment to propagandize publicly in support of "practices against procreation."[3]

As was also the case with his fellow fascist and partner in international crime, Adolph Hitler, the Italian dictator rationalized his expansionist adventures in Ethiopia (1935) and elsewhere by citing his nation's surplus population at the very same time he was extolling and encouraging rapid population growth. Ten years before the rape of Ethiopia a fascist senator, Count Antonio Cippico, while visiting the United States, crowed about Italy's desperate need for living space. He practically insisted that foreign countries absorb his nation's annual increment of a half million persons. Paradoxically, Mussolini, bent on reviving the glory of ancient Rome, announced a short time later that if Italy were to occupy her rightful place in the international community she would have to move into the second half of the twentieth century with a minimum of sixty million souls.[4] Il Duce's goal was highly ambitious as the Italian population according to a 1921 census was only thirty seven million.

Maximum Nordic multiplication was the chief objective of Nazi population policy. From the turn of the century to Hitler's accession to the chancellorship in 1933, Germany's birth rate had plunged. Although the actual population had increased by some nine million during that period of time, the leaders of the Third Reich were dissatisfied. To fulfill Germany's destiny cradles had to constantly exceed coffins. A swelling population meant enhanced national strength. Additional children meant additional battalions.

Nazi rhetoric was dotted with phrases such as "on the battle front."[5] German women were implored to do their duty to their race and their Fatherland, to be fruitful and to replenish the earth with good Germans. Propaganda Minister Joseph Goebbels declared that the mission of a woman was to be beautiful and to bear children.[6] "The woman has her own battlefield," Hitler himself told a Nazi women's congress in 1935. "With every child that she brings into the world, she fights her battle for the nation."[7] The Führer had little use for the egalitarian philosophy of feminism. In his view the mother of five or six or seven offspring had made more of a contribution than a female judge, and after June 1936 women were prohibited from being jurists. Minister of the Interior Wilhelm Frick even spoke of grading German women on the basis of their fertility.

A cult of motherhood was officially nourished. Prolific mothers were honored by the state on August 12, Hitler's mother's birthday. Starting in 1939 on that date, tribute was paid to those racially suitable German women whose output had been bountiful. They would be decorated with the "German Mother's Cross," no less a distinction than being invested with the Iron Cross.[8] A Nazi health official explained that the fecund German mother was to be granted the same place of honor as the combat soldier "since she risks her body and her life for the people and the Fatherland as much as the combat soldier does in the roar and thunder of battle."[9] Women who had begotten four offspring received a bronze medal. Women who had produced six earned a silver medal. A gold medal was reserved for the woman whose womb had brought forth at least eight specimens of the master race.

Procreation became an obsession in the Third Reich. It is significant that among the new words that entered the German lexicon in that era were *Gebärmaschinen* (child-bearing machine) and the foot and a half long *bevolkerungspolitische Blindganger* (eugenic duds). The first neologism denoted fruitful females, the second infertile ones.[10]

Inducement to breed in abundance was also provided by a marriage loan plan. An interest-free loan of a thousand Reichsmarks was made to newly married couples.[11] One-fourth of the loan, that is, two hundred and fifty Reichsmarks, would be canceled for each child born to the pair. When four offspring were produced, as Nazi demographic enthusiasts hoped would be the case, the original debt was completely paid off. Tax relief was also available to large families and there were subsidies for parents with many progeny. To qualify, however, they had to be healthy and of Aryan stock. Bundles of joy were called gifts to Hitler. They were future Nazis. They were tomorrow's warriors and the mothers of future warriors. A reich ordained to last a thousand years, especially one bidding for global hegemony, would require cannon fodder aplenty. The Austrian-born dictator could afford to be generous to those who were reproductively vigorous.

Yet another institution to promote propagation was the *Lebensborn* or "fount of life" association founded by the S.S. It operated a network of maternity houses not only for the benefit of procreative married mothers, but also for women giving birth to children out of wedlock. Some of the children were sired by the

S.S., in theory for dispassionate eugenic purposes. If the racial pedigrees of male and female were above reproach, barrenness was the sin, not illegitimacy.

Ilsa McKee, one-time member of a Hitler youth organization, has recalled lectures she attended on the need to elevate the German birth rate. Those lessons resulted in "quite a few illegitimate small sons and daughters for the Reich brought forth by teen age members . . . conceived in the grounds of our Hitler Youth Home." Believing that they had done what was expected of them, the young ladies were indifferent to the scandal.[12] The Nazis tried to eradicate the stigma attached to giving birth outside the conventional conjugal relationship. To that end the minister of the interior issued an edict stating that women bearing illegitimate children were henceforth to be called "Frau."[13]

Repressive methods were an intrinsic part of the government-sponsored pro-natalist campaign. Abortion laws were tightened and enforced more energetically by the Nazis. Physicians found guilty of interrupting pregnancies were subject to lengthy terms in prison. Under the Weimar republican regime which had preceded the Third Reich, convicted abortionists had usually been fined, not incarcerated. Anti-abortionists who glibly link legalization of abortion to Nazism, who compare abortion clinics with gas chambers, conveniently ignore the fact that the stringent abortion policy of the National Socialists is essentially the one they themselves advocate today. In their zeal to buttress their case, anti-abortionists often manifest symptoms of that age-old malady, selective historical amnesia.

Well worth remembering too is the fact that shortly after the Nazi takeover, contraceptive advertising, which had been commonplace in German magazines until then, vanished. Clinics dispensing birth control information were padlocked.[14] Free choice regarding parenthood was but one domestic casualty of the Hitler years.

Fascist doctrine in Italy and Germany clearly subordinated the well-being of individuals to the supreme needs of the state. Individual interests were recognized only insofar as they coincided with those of the state. Hordes of Teutonic supermen were deemed necessary by the Führer. Italian multitudes were deemed essential by Il Duce. Whether large broods were good for individual families was never even considered by Hitler or Mussolini. Such was the unfeeling, extremely chauvinistic totalitarian outlook.

Totalitarian states were not the only ones to adopt philoprogenitive policies in the period between the two world wars. They were not the only ones to make strength synonymous with numbers. France, long the most populous state in Europe, suffered a noticeable decline in its birth rate after the Franco-Prussian War of 1870-1871. Its European neighbors enjoyed proliferating populations while the French population advanced slowly. Contributing to the demographic stagnation was contraception, especially coitus interruptus, which was practiced widely. When coupling, French couples knew when to stop.

French losses in World War I—two million sacrificed their lives—alarmed the government of the Third Republic. In the hope of boosting the Gallic population, a law was passed in 1920 which forbade the spread of "contraceptive propaganda." Thereafter, new family planning clinics could not be opened. Even with this coercive element, even with substantial immigration in the interim, the French population in 1939 was little changed from what it had been a quarter of a century earlier. A family assistance plan first broached in the nineteenth century was finally adopted just prior to the Nazi invasion. Designed to encourage large families, the plan was successful in the aftermath of World War II. An upswing in the French birth rate was recorded with gratification and relief. To some the absence of a natural increase in the French population since 1900 had been disturbing evidence that decadence was ingrained in French society. Supposedly, the family assistance program proved them wrong. In addition, a more populous France meant a stronger, more glorious France.

Peoples who have suffered acute oppression continue to associate safety and security with inflated numbers. Jews are a good example. From time to time Jews are exhorted to be fruitful, to multiply, and to turn a deaf ear to all talk of a global population

explosion. They are told that the Jewish demographic situation is
unique. The Nazi holocaust meant a staggering population loss for
European Jewry which the Jews have the right, nay the obligation,
to regain. Six million perished. In 1974 Gilbert Klaperman, an
orthodox rabbi on Long Island, said that "Jews had a special right
to recoup their losses."[15] The late David Ben-Gurion, a founding
father of Israel and that nation's first prime minister, once wrote
that any fertile Jewish woman who does not bear at least four
healthy children is derelict in her duty to the Jewish nation. Her
dereliction was equated with that of the man who evades military
service.[16] Beleaguered by hostile neighbors, Israeli leaders believe
that their technological superiority is not enough to offset the great
numerical superiority of the Arabs. Arab citizens of Israel are
increasing at a fantastically swift pace and that too imperils the
Jewish character of the state. A Jewish majority is the sine qua non
of a Jewish nation. Ingathering of Jewish "exiles" from the
Diaspora is imperative both for Zionist ideological and security
reasons. Lifting the Israeli birth rate would reduce reliance on
*Aliya* (immigration).

The "more the better" demographic dogma notwithstanding,
American Jews are, by and large, very enthusiastic practitioners of
contraception. There is no talk of Gentiles liquidating Jews by
foisting birth control upon them, although it is noteworthy that
Margaret Sanger was accused by opponents of establishing her
clinic in New York City to "do away with the Jews."[17] There is
talk that the overwhelmingly middle-class American Jewish community, because it is reproductively lethargic, will do away with
itself.

There are roughly six million Jews in the United States. Had
Jews reproduced at the same pace as Gentile Americans since
World War II there would be a million and a half more Jews today.
But Jews were practicing zero population growth long before it
became either a slogan or a movement. To Milton Himmelfarb of
the American Jewish Committee, zero population growth gives
Hitler a "posthumous victory." Unborn Jews are no less a loss

than those who convert to Christianity, according to this line of thought.[18]

Some American Jews, fearing that intermarriage will lead to assimilation, have articulated a pro-natalist position. Before too long the Jewish culture will wither away. If the American Jewish community fails to grow, Rabbi Sol Roth, newly elected president of the New York Board of Rabbis, said in January 1974, "it will grow weaker and will face a threat to its extinction." Noting that the number of American Jews is about the same today as it was three decades ago, Rabbi Roth said that zero population growth was not applicable to American Jewry. The larger the family the better in his opinion, with three offspring the minimum for each Jewish family.[19]

Conspicuously more underprivileged than Jews in the United States are Hispanic minorities. They advance strength in size and genocide theories more than occasionally. About five million Americans of Mexican extraction comprise the largest contingent of Spanish-speaking citizens. Despised, lampooned, and discriminated against, Mexican-Americans have been known to comment that their bargaining position vis-à-vis the Anglo majority would be improved by the sheer weight of numbers. Recalling that past experimental contraceptive research has utilized Mexican-American subjects (sometimes without their full knowledge), some Chicanos have perceived a plot to attenuate the power of *la raza*. There may well be a consensus among Chicanos that the perils of overpopulation have been exaggerated by the white establishment.[20] Powerless and poor for so long, Mexican-Americans, or at least some of their spokesmen, believe that a larger community would be so powerful that its interests could not be ignored. Manuel Aragon, Jr., a respected Californian, currently a deputy mayor of Los Angeles, told the Commission on Population Growth and the American Future in May 1971 that large Mexican-American families must be encouraged "so that we will eventually be so numerous that the system will either respond or it will be overwhelmed."[21]

On the zero population growth issue, Joe C. Ortega, a staff counsel for the Mexican-American Legal Defense and Educational Fund, has found his people simultaneously pulled in opposite directions. Fewer Chicanos would mean more jobs and a fairer share of America's wealth. On the other hand, zero population growth could undermine the deeply rooted traditions of a close, large family. Under present conditions, the farm labor economy favors larger families. All from the age of seven pick cotton and other crops.

In the barrios of Tucson, Arizona, San Antonio, Texas, and East Los Angeles tuberculosis is still a scourge. Life expectancy is appallingly low and infant mortality distressingly high. Survival is a never-ending struggle. Under such conditions population control has little meaning. "In the hierarchy of values and priorities of the Nation," Ortega has said "[zero population growth] is not as important as equality, justice and liberty—commodities which the Mexican-American has yet to receive in any quantity, much less abundance." Until the Chicano starts to enjoy the health and well-being enjoyed by the Anglo, he will not actively participate in population control. Only when he becomes middle class will he adopt middle-class values including small families, Ortega has prophesied. [22]

The power through population growth argument and the companion genocide allegation have both been heard in the squalid barrios of the Puerto Rican community. Among the approximately one and a half million Puerto Ricans on the mainland, the most strident voices on these touchy issues have been those of the Young Lords. Initially a street gang, later a revolutionary political organization, the Young Lords have often been compared to the Black Panthers. *Palante*, the newspaper of the Young Lords, in January 1971 criticized American television for its silence on "how doctors tell us to take the pill, making us believe that it is safe, when in fact they were using us as guinea pigs and all the time making us sterile." [23] Puerto Ricans interviewed in recent years have exhibited irritation over the fact that before contraceptive pills were officially approved for use on the mainland, they were tried out in Puerto Rico.[24]

In October 1974 Juan Mari Bras, secretary-general of the Puerto Rican Socialist party and an advocate of independence, told the United Nations' twenty-four country special committee on colonialism that "North American imperialists" had launched a genocidal plan in Puerto Rico. More than two hundred thousand women, more than a third of the island's women of child-bearing age, had been sterilized. What Señor Bras neglected to tell the UN was that Puerto Rico's free sterilization program was entirely voluntary, that it was endorsed overwhelmingly by the local population, and that a substantial number of the women sterilized already had more than four children. What Señor Bras also failed to tell the world body was that currently Puerto Rico is more thickly settled than India, China, or Japan. If Puerto Rico were to "enjoy" a natural growth rate of 2 percent, by the year 2000 its density would be comparable to squeezing double the world's present population into the United States.

Puerto Rican groups favoring independence for their crowded Caribbean island rather than the existing commonwealth status insist that an independent, sovereign Puerto Rican state would benefit from and could support a still larger population. Power and political leverage are equated with more bodies, an equation which is dubious at best.

If any minority in this country has good historical reason to fear extermination, it is the red American. Almost from the day European explorers first set foot in the New World, his saga has been one of unending tribulation. White efforts to commit genocide against the indigenous occupants of the continent were myriad and need not be recounted here. Yet the present generation of American Indians does not appear to regard birth control as part of the pattern of decimation. Nor has deliberate rejection of birth control by native Americans to enhance their strength and influence been encountered by researchers.[25]

There are notable exceptions, however. Russell Means of AIM, the militant American Indian Movement and a leader in the 1973 takeover of Wounded Knee, South Dakota, is one exception. To him birth control is genocidal as are all United States government programs for his people. He has stated emphatically that American Indian girls are involuntarily and unnecessarily sterilized on reservations "all the time."[26] For "spiritual" rather than tactical reasons, "birth is the natural order of things." Means believes that the more Indian babies that are born the better. He proudly asserts that native Americans are the fastest growing ethnic group in what he often refers to as "Nazi America."[27]

Problems of overpopulation do not seem to be a cause of sleeplessness among Indian spokesmen. In a recent book, Lame Deer, a Sioux medicine man, told about having asked ten of his best Indian friends for an opinion about "birth control." Nine had replied that it was "no good" and the tenth was a "wino." Lame Deer added:

> The population explosion doesn't worry us much. All these long years, when the only good Indian was a dead Indian, the bodies at Wounded Knee, the Sand Creek Massacre, the Washita, all this killing of women and children, the measles and smallpox, wiping out whole tribes—the way I see it, the Indians have done all the population control one could ask of them a hundred times over. Our problem is survival. Over-population—that's your worry.[28]

Against the sordid backdrop of the white man's butchery of the red man, Lame Deer is claiming that Indians ought to be exempt from the responsibilities incumbent upon all groups and individuals to combat overpopulation. His claim is very similar to that invoked by Jews against the background of the Nazi holocaust. While parochial and self-serving, such claims are not difficult to understand.

Despite the fact that Indian life expectancy is still twenty-three years less than that for other Americans; despite the fact that the Indian suicide rate is almost two times higher than that for the general population; despite the fact that the Indian's infant mortality rate is 24 percent higher and the Indian's maternal death rate is almost double that for all other races; despite all of these statistical truths the red American is not about to vanish.[29] According to the 1970 decennial census there were 791,839 Indians living in the United States. This total was 50 percent higher than that for 1960. Native Americans are, in fact, increasing their numbers at almost four times the pace of their fellow, but more privileged, citizens. There has even been facetious speculation by one wag that if the first Americans continue to multiply as rapidly as they did between 1950 and 1970, while the demographic trend for other Americans approaches zero population growth, "by about the year 3000 there would be a hundred million Indians—conceivably enough to try to take the country back."[30]

Accusations of "twisted neo-Malthusian plans," of racial genocidal conspiracies, and of the political misuse of birth control have intermittently been hurled at the United States by Latin Americans.[31] These accusations, interestingly enough, come from leftists, Marxist and non-Marxist alike; from conservative nationalists; and from Roman Catholic clerics. Mistrust of the Anglo-Saxon colossus to the north is a common theme in the expressions of opposition to family planning and population control. United States penetration of Latin American economies, particularly the domination of certain key extractive mineral industries, is deeply resented. By containing population growth in South American countries, industrialized, technologically advanced nations led by the United States can continue to dominate them economically, it is suggested. Imperialists fronting for rapacious American vendors of birth control pills are behind the needless worry about runaway population growth, says Colombian José Consuegra. Latin America already has the highest population growth rate in the world, 3 percent annually, but the continent could comfortably accommodate fifty times its present population, declares Consuegra, a left-wing economist.[32]

More than one intellectual south of the border believes racism is also a motive underlying the actions of gringo family planners.

Darcy Ribiero, a former minister of education in Brazil, has written that the racially mixed populace of Latin America has a unique role to play in future history. Further miscegenation will produce a "more homogeneous type of human being, who will possess a greater aptitude for living with and identifying with all peoples." That prospect fills white supremacists with dread, says Ribiero. "If the Anglo Americans succeed in this proposition of reducing the Black population and the mixed contingents of Latin America by imposing a policy of demographic containment, the result will be a fortification of heterogeneity and racism."[33]

El Salvador's Napoleon Viera Altamirano has been called "Latin America's most articulate pro-natalist."[34] In one of his many editorial diatribes against family planning, Altamirano, a crusading conservative nationalist, identifies a bewildering medley of villains. The United States does not always occupy center stage. There are Europeans and others who are disturbed by so many "negroes, [sic] indians, [sic] mulattos, [sic] and mestizos." There are people who want to prevent the "Central American man from taking possession of his land." Leftist interests are also deeply involved. Brimming with paranoia, Altamirano has conjured up a "vast racist communist and imperialist conspiracy . . . to socialize, depopulate and de-Catholicize us."[35]

Many Latin American advocates of rapid population growth categorically reject the notion that their poverty is due to an excess of people. Instead, they say, antiquated social and economic institutions are to blame. Often it is declared that South America is too sparsely settled and that underpopulation has actually curbed economic development.

Mexico's National Union of Heads of Families has taken issue with the government's belated efforts to decelerate Mexico's cancerous population growth and has declared that Mexico does not have an excess of people. Indeed, she could do with more people to exploit her natural resources.[36] Peruvians too have been known to make such declarations, and so have Argentinians and Brazilians.

In March 1974 Argentinian government officials announced their intention to double their country's population by the year 2000. Argentina, with a land mass approximately as large as that of India, has a total population of twenty-five million, a fraction of India's. In a veiled reference to Argentina's chief continental rival, Brazil, the magazine *Las Bases* predicted that at the beginning of the twenty-first century "we will have overpopulated neighbors with great food problems, and we . . . will have three million square kilometers of land, practically unpopulated. We will not have the arms to work this immense and rich territory and if we do not do it there will be others who will." *Las Bases* usually reflected the thinking of the late Argentinian President Juan Domingo Perón.[37] Perón's widow who succeeded him has pledged not to deviate one iota from her late husband's policies.

To meet the demographic challenge, stern measures were planned by the Perón regime. Oral contraceptives were to be made difficult to procure. The spread of information about family planning was to be halted entirely and Argentinians were to be educated to appreciate the supposed dangers of practicing contraception. [38]

The Juan Perón government took a conspiratorial view of the population problem. Unidentified "non-Argentine interests" were charged with fostering birth control and with subverting the paramount function of women, namely maternity. A foreign foundation was upbraided for financing the voluntary sterilization of Argentinian women. Again no name was given.[39]

Unlike Argentina which is overwhelmingly European, Brazil is, in the main, a mulatto nation. Indeed, it is not inconceivable that Argentinian anxiety about their Portuguese-speaking rival may be racially tinged. Seen in the light of the Argentinian attitudes, it is perhaps ironic that there are Brazilian pundits who think that their country, the fifth largest in area in the entire world (larger than the United States excluding Alaska) and the fastest rising economic power in South America, is underpopulated. The fact that approximately half of Brazil's land is jungle is glossed over. Brazil with a population of roughly 92,237,000 in 1970 ranks eighth in the world. A population of two hundred million is projected for the year 2000.

In Brazil as in Argentina some individuals who should know better say that a quick growing population encourages rather than retards economic development. In Brazil as in Argentina some individuals who should know better say that the wealthier, developed nations are scheming to keep the poorer, developing nations in a dependent, subordinate position by pushing birth control.

In 1967 foreign missionaries were accused of sterilizing Brazilian women. They were guilty of "genocide," the objective of which was lowering the population of Brazil. Outsiders, it was said, wanted to colonize Brazilian land which they had first to depopulate.[40]

Planned parenthood is promoted in Brazil by a private nonprofit family planning agency, the Society for Family Welfare in Brazil, or Benfam for short. Unlike the Peronists in Argentina, the government of Brazil does not interfere with Benfam's birth control operations. Neither does it endorse those operations. However, of late, some figures in the national government have sanctioned the idea of family planning for Brazilians, and local governments have signed contracts with Benfam calling for the establishment of family planning clinics.[41]

Enthusiastic government support for family planning is not likely to materialize in the near future. Chauvinists in Brazil like those elsewhere will continue to define national destiny in terms of strength, which they mistakenly believe is synonymous with more bodies, and not in terms of a high literacy rate or a low incidence of infant mortality—in other words, not in humanitarian terms.

Third World leaders are, in many cases, more inclined to see burgeoning populations as a national asset rather than as a national liability. Obviously, India's Indira Gandhi labors under no such illusion. But Algeria's President Houari Boumedienne has described the enormous population of nonaligned developing states as "the Third World's atom bomb."[42] This is a callous view when famine is casting an ever-lengthening global shadow. Between four hundred million and five hundred million children in have-not countries are threatened by severe malnutrition, even starvation, the executive director of the United Nations Children's Fund warned in May 1974.[43] At any given moment, millions of infants are suffering from malnutrition which could cause irreversible mental retardation. Atom bomb indeed!

Marxist thinking has had an unfortunate impact on some Third World demographic ideas. Marxists have long agreed that exploitation, and not an excess of people, represents the real stumbling block to economic health and well-being. Poverty, unemployment, and "overpopulation" have been the bitter fruits of capitalism. A socialist regime, it is argued, could cope with any increase in population. So argued the delegate from the Soviet Union to the United Nations Population Commission in 1947. Capitalism is the villain, communism the panacea. Talk of overpopulation is considered a diversionary tactic.

A mimeographed handout of the Progressive Labor party in this country has called the "too many people" argument advanced by the zero population growth school "racist hysteria." Concisely stated, the Maoist Progressive Labor party position is that the "problem of nonwhite people whether outside or inside the United States is super-exploitation and racist oppression, not 'overpopulation'."[44] It does not even occur to these monomaniacal analysts of the nonwhite's dilemmas in a white-dominated world that the problem could be both.

Curiously, Mao, while not emphatically repudiating the Marxist-Leninist line that the population problem is a matter of capitalist greed and inequitable distribution of the world's resources, has now ordered drastic measures to check the Chinese birth rate. As many as eight hundred million persons are inhabitants of what we now respectfully refer to as the People's Republic of China. Marx and Lenin notwithstanding, as early as the 1950s the red mandarin rulers of China were retreating by stages from the pro-natalist Communist ideology. By 1974

Peking had decided that two children per family were sufficient. To deter Chinese couples from reproducing further, the government in the future will withhold various maternal benefits. It is even prepared to deny the third child a household registration certificate, an action which makes the redundant infant a nonperson.[45] Is it conceivable that the Progressive Labor party comrades in the United States are more Maoist than Mao, who has revealed himself to be a rank deviationist in his population policies?

## NOTES

1. R. Sauer, "Attitudes to Abortion in America 1800-1973," *Population Studies* 28, No. 1 (March 1974): 59. John T. Noonan, Jr., *Contraception—A History of Its Treatment by the Catholic Theologians and Canonists* (New York: A Mentor-Omega Book, 1967), pp. 488-489.

2. Alexander Robertson, *Mussolini and the New Italy* (New York: Fleming H. Revell Co., 1928), p. 152.

3. Noonan, *Contraception*, p. 489.

4. Margaret Sanger, *Margaret Sanger—An Autobiography* (New York: W. W. Norton and Co. Publishers, 1938), p. 377.

5. Hans Peter Bleuel, *Sex and Society in Nazi Germany*, trans. J. Maxwell Brownjohn (Philadelphia: J. B. Lippincott Co., 1973), p. 149.

6. George L. Mosse, *Nazi Culture—Intellectual, Cultural and Social Life in the Third Reich* (New York: Grosset & Dunlap, 1966), p. 41.

7. Ibid., p. 40.

8. Bleuel, *Sex and Society in Nazi Germany*, p. 153.

9. Quoted in Mosse, *Nazi Culture*, p. 45.

10. Richard Grünberger, *The 12-Year Reich—A Social History of Nazi Germany* (New York: Holt, Rinehart and Winston Inc., 1971), p. 242.

11. The amount of the loans was subsequently reduced to five hundred Reichsmarks.

12. Ilse McKee, *Tomorrow The World* (London: J. M. Dent & Sons, Ltd., 1960), p. 9.

13. Grünberger, *The 12-Year Reich*, p. 246.

14. Clifford Kirkpatrick, *Nazi Germany: Its Women and Family Life* (Indianapolis: The Bobbs-Merrill Co., 1938) pp. 160-162.

15. *New York Times*, 24 January 1974. On Jewish demography, see Allen S. Maller, "The Population Crisis and the Jewish People, *Congress Bi-Weekly*, 12 November 1971, pp. 13-14; Moses D. Tendler, "Population Control—The Jewish View," *Tradition* 8, No. 3 (Fall 1966): 5-14. Tendler also makes the orthodox Jewish case against population control techniques on religious grounds. Relevant is Milton Himmelfarb, "A Plague of Children," *Commentary*, April 1971, pp. 37-43, and Norman Podhoretz, "Speak of the Devil," (p. 6) in the same issue of *Commentary*. Also useful is Marc Holzer, "ZPG: A Jewish Concern," *Congress Bi-Weekly*, 9 November 1973, pp. 12-14.

16. David Ben-Gurion, *Israel—A Personal History* (New York: Funk and Wagnalls, Inc., 1971), p. 839.

17. Sanger, *Margaret Sanger—An Autobiography*, p. 226.

18. Quoted in Kathie Sutin, *1.5 M.U.S. Jews Lost by ZPG Since 1940, The Jewish Post and Opinion*, 19 April 1974, p. 1.

19. *New York Times*, 24 January 1974.

20. This was one finding of a California study on black, white, and Mexican-American thinking about fertility control. See Robert Buckhout, "Toward a Two-Child Norm: Changing Family Planning Attitudes," *American Psychologist* 27 (1972): 22.

21. U.S. Commission on Population Growth and the American Future, *Statements at Public Hearings of the Commission on Population Growth and the American Future*, Volume VII of Commission Publications (Washington, D.C.: U.S. Government Printing Office, 1972), p. 81.

22. Joe C. Ortega, letter to the author, 26 March 1974. Mr. Ortega expressed many of these views before a U.S. Senate Committee studying population problems.

23. Quoted in Donald P. Warwick and Nancy Williamson, "Population Policy and Spanish Speaking Americans," Unpublished paper prepared for the Population Task Force of the Institute for Society, Ethics and the Life Sciences as part of its study for the Commission on Population Growth and the American Future, August 1971, p. 4.

24. Ibid., pp. 18-19.

25. Emily C. Moore, "Native American Indian Values: Their Relation to Suggested Population Policy Proposals," Unpublished paper prepared

for the Population Task Force of the Institute for Society, Ethics, and the Life Sciences as part of its study for the Commission on Population Growth and the American Future (n.d.).

26. Russell Means, personal interview, 11 May 1974.

27. Ibid.

28. John Fire/Lame Deer and Richard Erdoes, *Lame Deer—Seeker of Visions* (New York: Simon and Schuster, 1972), p. 153.

29. These data were provided by the director of the Indian Health Service, U.S. Department of Health, Education and Welfare.

30. E. J. Kahn, Jr., "A Reporter at Large—Who, What, Where, How Much, How Many?" Part II. *The New Yorker*, 22 October 1973.

31. See Jordan Bishop, "Imperialism and the Pill," *Commonweal, 10* January 1969, pp. 465-467; Thomas G. Sanders, *Opposition to Family Planning in Latin America: The Non-Marxist Left*, American Universities Field Staff Reports, West Coast South America Series XVII, No. 5 (March 1970).

32. José Consuegra, *El Control de la Natalidad Como Arma del Imperialismo* (Buenos Aires: Editorial Galerna, 1969).

33. Quoted in Sanders, *Opposition to Family Planning in Latin America*, p. 3.

34. J. Mayone Stycos, "Opposition to Family Planning in Latin America: Conservative Nationalism," *Demography* 5, No. 2 (1968): 849.

35. Ibid., 851.

36. *New York Times*, 27 May 1974. Also see Marvin Alisky, "Mexico Versus Malthus: National Trends," *Current History*, May 1974, pp. 200 ff.

37. Jonathan Kandell, "Argentina, Hoping to Double Her Population This Century, Is Taking Action to Restrict Birth Control," *New York Times*, 17 March 1974.

38. Ibid.

39. Ibid.

40. Thomas G. Sanders, *The Politics of Population in Brazil*, American Universities Field Staff Reports, East Coast South America Series XV, No. 1 (1971): 6.

41. Walter Rodriguez, "Family Planning: Hope for a Nation," in *Population and Family Planning in Latin America*, Report #17 (Washington, D.C.: Victor Bostrom Fund, 1973), pp. 20-22.

42. Quoted in C. Z. Sulzberger, "Subterranean Politics," *New York Times*, 9 January 1974.

43. *New York Times*, 14 May 1974.

44. "ZPG: A Fascist Movement! A Progressive Labor Party Position," in Daniel Callahan (ed.), *The American Population Debate* (Garden City: Anchor Books, 1971), pp. 68-76.

45. *Providence Sunday Journal*, 24 March 1974.

# 6. *Strength in Numbers in the Black World*

On the African continent, historical, racial, and national factors appear to color perceptions of population questions to a greater degree than do Marxist teachings. Disquietude about its neighbors, especially Guinea and Ghana, helps to clarify the tepid response of government leaders in the Ivory Coast to family planning. Trained as a physician, President Houphouet-Boigny is alive to the benefits of planned parenthood, but is hesitant to back any program that might weaken his country numerically or otherwise vis-à-vis other West African countries. His ambivalence on the matter is reflected in the anomalous situation wherein contraceptives are relatively easy to obtain but the dissemination of family planning information is illegal.[1] Also militating against family planning is the Ivoirien uneasiness that it would enable alien Africans living in their country to outbreed bona fide citizens of the Ivory Coast.

Overpopulation is not a weighty problem in black Africa, or so it is believed by some in West African states. An opinion survey on population and family planning showed this to be the case in Francophone Senegal and Anglophone Nigeria.[2] There it was thought that more people, especially skilled people, would expedite economic development.

Hastings Kamazu Banda, president for life of the central African nation of Malawi, formerly Nyasaland, sees greater glory for his country if its population multiplies rapidly. Banda, a moderate—some would say a "sell-out"—in the spectrum of independent African politics, talks about doubling the Malawi population. He has done more than talk. He has outlawed the dispensing of contraceptive information and devices, despite the fact that jobless citizens of Malawi must trek to the Republic of South Africa for work. Very densely populated, Malawi is already one of the poorest nations in the world, a situation which Banda's opposition to planned parenthood and population planning can only aggravate.[3]

Skeptical rumblings about the advertised objectives of population policies initiated by foreigners have also emanated from black Africa. A headline in a Uganda publication in the mid-1960s read "Family Planning Is Murder." In that east African country and elsewhere (including the United States), planned parenthood and population control are assumed to be identical, a confusion which works to the distinct disadvantage of the family planning movement.[4]

A few years ago a Nigerian newspaperman bluntly asserted that the "idea of family planning as peddled by the Euro-American world is an attempt to keep Africa weak." Nigeria, with just under eighty million people according to the most recent census, is easily the most populous country on the African continent. Relatively few governments in sovereign sub-Saharan nations share the Nigerian journalist's jaundiced view of family planning. Still, mistrust of the white world is an important component of the legacy left to Africa by the slave traders and the European imperialists. When the more developed, richer, white nations, in effect, tell underdeveloped, poorer, black nations to limit their reproduction, the latter understandably interpret this as a manifestation of neocolonialism, racism, or Yankee imperialism. Population biologist Paul Ehrlich, a rabid advocate of zero population growth to avert global disaster, has stated: "Until it's perfectly clear that we're going to give them a share of the world we want them to help save, there's going to be very little interest in real population control in many of the underdeveloped countries.''[5]

Overpopulation and ecology must be the furthest thing from the minds of black Africans in the unfree white redoubt of southern Africa where their basic rights are severely circumscribed. How can they not wonder why their white rulers assiduously promote European immigration while they simultaneously encourage birth control in the black townships? This is the case in Rhodesia where approximately two hundred and fifty thousand Europeans dominate an African population which now outnumbers them twenty to one. Glossy brochures stressing the golden sunshine and plentiful land were an integral part of the white Rhodesian government's ''Settler '74'' campaign to lure European immigrants. In this context Africans in Rhodesia, or Zimbabwe as they prefer to call their country, have denounced family planning as a government instrument to reduce the voting strength of non-Europeans. Radio Zambia, in its attacks on family planning in Rhodesia, also focuses on the franchise issue.[6] Bantu politicos in Zimbabwe itself often argue that having children is a political activity. ''We will smother the Europeans with our children,'' is the recurring theme in these arguments. Census data lend some credence to their arguments. In a single year, 1969, the number of African infants born in Rhodesia (215,000) almost equaled the total European population.[7] The black population is climbing at breakneck speed but it is heralding much suffering rather than hastening deliverance from European control.

Much the same situation exists south of the Limpopo River in the Republic of South Africa. There the reins of power are held tightly by the roughly four million whites, persons mostly of Dutch and English ancestry. Almost eighteen million Bantu and in excess of two million Coloured, the name South Africa gives to its racially mixed population, are at the mercy of their white suzerains. Rigid racial segregation or apartheid (pronounced apart-hate) is not merely tolerated. It is mandated. It is the law of the land. Nonwhites enjoy only those political, social, and economic rights which the ruling minority deigns to confer upon them.

Family planners in South Africa report that the question of genocide has cropped up from time to time over the years. Newspaper articles and letters to the editor appear occasionally but the Family Planning Association of South Africa does not consider the issue to be a serious one. Birth control is often warmly received by individual African women; also, Bantu leaders, such as Chief Minister C. N. Phatudi of the Bantu homeland of Lebowa, believe that by limiting their growth Africans as a people will grow stronger.

Yet in the urban areas some Africans see multiplication as a defense against the white supremacist Afrikaner government which tries to entice new European settlers and, at the same time, operates a national family planning program with "non-Europeans" especially in mind. Significantly, the private Family Planning Association does not talk of population control in South Africa. With the country's multiracial population such talk would be dynamite, it concedes. The association does argue that child-spacing is good for the entire family, that parents should aim to produce quality, not quantity, and that all races can profit from this family planning philosophy—all seemingly irrefutable arguments.[8] But, because of his overall predicament, the African's credulity is stretched somewhat.

Black fears that birth control is a white plot to kill off people of African descent are not confined to Africa or the United States. They have surfaced in the Caribbean, particularly in Jamaica, the largest and most populous of the former British West Indian islands. About fifteen years ago, in the opinion of the Jamaica Family Planning Association, the genocide issue was a serious barrier to the acceptance of family planning. Today, however, it appears to be among the least significant expressed objections, well below objections based on religious scruples, superstitious ideas, and health notions.[9]

Pockets of resistance remain however, notably among the Rastafarians, an exotic, messianic cult. Although the "Rastas" are somewhat heterogeneous in doctrine, they share certain fundamental tenets. The two principal ones are (1) that Emperor Haile Selassie of Ethiopia is the living God, the returned messiah, and (2) that they are destined to be repatriated to their African homeland. According to the author of the most thorough study of the Rastafarians, they also subscribe to the belief that Caucasians are scheming through the use of birth control to destroy "God's people," i.e., black men.[10] Ideology grounded in the Biblical prophecy that the "seeds of Israel must be numberless" also predisposes this religious black nationalist movement to reject birth control.

Rastafarians made their position clear to family planning authorities in a 1968 meeting. They would not permit their queens (wives) "to be mingled with or interfered with by a physician." Overpopulation did not trouble them. Catastrophes, natural or man-made, would take care of surplus populations. If Jamaica suffered from a shortage of space, the Rastas should be dispatched to Africa. Birth control was homicide, they told the family planning officials at the meeting which was held in Montego Bay, on Jamaica's beautiful north coast. Preventing births was like killing God. Family planning was more menacing than the atomic bomb. One Rasta announced defiantly that he already had four children and planned on fathering twenty-five more if possible. Throughout the encounter the Rastafarians were belligerent. They finally stalked out of the meeting.[11]

Talk about strength in numbers or genocide is almost never heard on Barbados, the easternmost of the sundrenched Caribbean islands. Although the former British dependency has been exporting people for over a century, it is still one of the most densely populated countries in the world and expects to double its population of almost a quarter million by the year 2002.[12] Population control there is not a luxury. It is an absolute necessity. Harsh geographic realities leave little room for ideological delusions.

Planned parenthood as a concept and as a movement enjoys the unqualified support of Prime Minister Errol Barrow's government, which would prefer not to rely entirely on emigration as a safety valve. In September 1972 Barrow suggested that family planning education be given to children as young as ten.[13] The Barbados Family Planning Association, which has been in existence since 1955, operates with the government's blessings. In explaining the public's acceptance of family planning—that term is preferred to birth control—the president of the Barbados Family Planning Association listed the ministate's high literacy rate, the absence of overt racial friction, and the fact that his program is directed by blacks.[14]

Barbados' demographic enlightenment is not shared on Dominica, a poor island still associated with Britain. There Minister of Education and Health H. Christian announced in January 1973 that Dominica had no population explosion dilemma and would not be importing any foreign birth control system. Nor would he sanction legalized abortions on the island which is a predominantly Roman Catholic country.[15]

Ostensibly, the population problem of each West Indian island is unique and is shaped by a variety of factors, not the least important of which is the racial makeup of its people. On Trinidad the demographic picture is complicated by the presence of two large rival nonwhite groups, one with its roots in Africa, the other originating on the Indian subcontinent. Descendants of black slaves and of indentured Asian servants introduced into the island's sugar economy after Negro emancipation now vie for dominance in an atmosphere permeated by mutual mistrust. Family planning by the blacks could eventuate in political hegemony by East Indians who are, in general, loath to limit their family size.

Trinidadians are leery of planned parenthood for another reason. Earl Augustus, project director of the United Nations' Fund for Population Activities, told a teachers' seminar, "that there is some deep-rooted reservation which views family planning as a tool engineered by European powers for uncertain applications among Third World Peoples."[16] Revolutionary groups in Trinidad such as the National Joint Action Committee (NJAC) express this reservation most acidulously. An NJAC pamphlet laments the fact that everywhere Trinidadians turn there is a poster or advertisement urging them to reduce the number of children they are having, imploring them to use the pill. The NJAC sees this as an attack by a wicked establishment which exploits the country's resources and its people, the rightful owners of those resources.

Exploitation, not overpopulation, is *the* problem. Therefore, the solution cannot be fewer children. This monistic interpretation is characteristic of radical critiques of planned parenthood and population control. That overpopulation and maldistribution of wealth could both be problems seems not to occur to the NJAC. When the masses take what a small white elite and its nonwhite lackeys now greedily monopolize, Trinidad will be trouble-free. Nature will set no limits to agricultural abundance in this tropical paradise. There will be a cornucopia of food. People will be able to have as many offspring as they wish and will be able to feed them all. So runs the quixotic reasoning of the NJAC. But family planners are not really concerned with the people, says the revolutionary NJAC. They are "busy shoving all sorts of ideas down our throats about 'unwanted babies,' ideas like 'decorate your house this Christmas'—instead of having another child this year; all sorts of materialistic ideas." Throughout the Third World, have-not sable people were being subjected to this "new white mentality." Meanwhile white nations sucked the national wealth of the black world dry.[17]

For many black opponents of fertility limitation in the United States, the remarkably durable "strength in numbers" argument remains the most persuasive. "Our safety, our survival literally, depends on our ever increasing numbers and the heavy concentration of our people in the financial heart of America— namely in the large urban centers." So editorialized black nationalist Daniel H. Watts, an architect by training, who published the *Liberator*, a monthly journal now defunct. Rejecting the idea that there is any paucity of space or shortage of food in the United States, a country with allegedly forty million white racists, Watts has written that one of the best warrantees of black survival is "a more vigorous effort on our part to reproduce our own." Speaking in support of birth control for black Americans is tantamount to speaking in support of genocide.[18]

Numbers are also reassuring to Roy Innis, national director of CORE. Innis, a Virgin Islander by birth, has presided over the transformation of CORE from a one-time pacifist-based, interracial, integrationist-minded civil rights organization into a thoroughgoing black nationalist group. He believes that Afro-Americans would be a more formidable element on the American scene if they constituted a higher percentage of the nation's population. He associates Communist China's emergence as a superpower with her teeming millions. One out of every four human beings is Chinese. But Innis does confess to having ambivalent feelings about population questions. If contraceptives and abortions are accessible to whites, they should also be available to blacks. Because he is fearful of coercion—he has said that he knows of cases where undue pressure has been exerted on blacks—he wants birth control facilities to be operated by blacks themselves.[19]

There is nothing ambivalent about other black expressions of their faith in unrestricted reproduction. A black physician in Pittsburgh put it this way: "Our birth rate is the only thing we have. If we keep on producing they're going to have to either kill us or grant us full citizenship." One of the stated goals of the pro-natalist EROS (Endeavor to Raise Our Size), a California-based group, has been to increase the voting power of Afro-Americans. Walter Thompson, head of EROS, told a family planning worker that he was opposed to governmental financing of birth control services and was hostile to the Planned Parenthood agency which he wanted to destroy.[20]

A black member of the South Carolina state legislature, who had been elected by an overwhelmingly black constituency, told his supporters that if black Americans wanted to overcome, they should go ahead and have their babies. A spokesman for the Five Percenters, a little known black splinter organization in New York City, envisioned the uses of an inflated black population a little differently. As told in an *Ebony* article, he pointed to a pregnant black girl and remarked, "She's having another baby for me. I need an army and this is how we're going to get it." [21] In sum, the line of argument is that whether future blacks function within the political system or act to undermine it, greater numbers will be a help, not a hindrance.

Demographic changes have probably given the old numbers game new vitality. The percentage of blacks in the United States population declined steadily from 19.0 in 1810 to 9.7 in 1930. In absolute numbers the black population had increased from 757,208 in 1790 to 11,891,143 in 1930, but owing to the legislative termination of the Atlantic slave trade (which sharply reduced the importation of slaves, even if it did not actually end it) and to the European immigration to the United States, the proportion of persons of African extraction decreased.

Since 1930 when the effects of restrictive immigration laws were reflected in the ten-year census required by the Constitution, the percentage of blacks has risen, but not dramatically. In fact, in the first seven decades of this century the percentage of black Americans has remained about the same. In 1900 there were 8.8 million Negroes who represented roughly 12 percent of the United States population. As of 1971 the official black population was around 23 million, about 11 percent of the general population, up 0.2 percent from 1965. On July 1, 1973, the new estimated black population was 23.8 million out of a total United States population of 210,404,000. [22]

Blacks frequently scoff at these figures, contending that they are routinely undercounted. Every chance he gets Dick Gregory states publicly that he disbelieves the census statistics published by the government. James Forman among others claims that the black population is actually in excess of thirty million. Forman, of course, is best known for a May 1969 incident in which he interrupted religious worship at the Riverside Church in New York City to publicize his demand that reparations be paid to black Americans.

The Census Bureau has conceded that 5.3 million Americans

were not counted in the decennial census of 1970. The underenumeration of blacks was estimated at 1.88 million or 7.7 percent as compared with the Caucasian undercount put at 3.45 million or 1.9 percent.[23]

To maximize the accuracy of the 1970 headcount among minority groups, the Bureau of the Census made use of various techniques. It attempted to recruit local people as enumerators. It also launched community education programs to explain the importance of the census in minority neighborhoods. Aid from the federal government is allocated on a per capita basis. Thus money desperately needed for schools, health projects, and the like can be lost as a result of blacks being undercounted. Electoral districting and political representation are also linked with census data. Blacks not included in the census are therefore shortchanging themselves. To convey this message to the man on the ghetto streetcorner, the Bureau of the Census collaborated with several black organizations, but to little avail. Some census takers out of laziness or nervousness may have given certain central city tenements a wide berth. Some suspicious black ghetto dwellers undoubtedly dodged the census enumerator, mistaking him for a bill collector, a tax agent, or a plainclothes lawman. Still others reacted negatively to inquisitive strangers asking personal questions that seemed to be none of their business. It is entirely possible that the undercount of Afro-Americans is even more substantial than the Census Bureau admits.

Perhaps more meaningful than the total black American population is its distribution. According to the Census Bureau, blacks now constitute a clear majority in six cities including Newark, New Jersey, Washington, D.C., and Atlanta, Georgia. Eight additional cities have a population that is 40 percent black. These phenomena are attributable in large measure to a white exodus from the rotting inner cities. In any case 50 percent of America's blacks are to be found in fifty cities and one-third of the total black population is concentrated in just fifteen cities.

Do these figures warrant Daniel Watts' conclusion that the "city has become the Black man's land"? By virtue of their size black communities have managed to elect mayors in Gary, Indiana; Cleveland; Newark; Raleigh, North Carolina; Dayton, Ohio; Grand Rapids, Michigan; Detroit; Los Angeles; Atlanta; and elsewhere. But whether the quality of life for black residents of those urban centers has improved, even slightly, is debatable. The crucial economic relationship between whites and blacks has not really been altered.

Formidable, possibly insurmountable, barriers confront the black mayor chosen by a largely black electorate. More often than not, he is elected to govern a municipality which is in its death throes. Middle-class whites, the backbone of the economy, have taken flight. Crime is rampant, housing is decaying. The treasury is nearly depleted. To make matters worse the long-deferred hopes of the inner-city blacks have been elevated unrealistically by the election of one of their own kind.[24]

And this is no age of miracles, as Kenneth Gibson of Newark knows all too well. In 1970 Gibson, an engineer by training, became the first black American to be elected mayor of a major eastern seaboard city. All of Newark's residents, regardless of race, have benefited from the fact that Gibson restored integrity to city hall in short order. For the first time blacks were given a sense of participation in the political life of the city. Black attorneys were appointed to the bench and blacks achieved policy-making positions in the educational system.

Gibson has been able to obtain money from the federal government, but his administration has been far from a bonanza for his black constituents. Unemployment and underemployment of blacks in Newark are well above the national average for blacks. Drug addiction is close to epidemic proportions. Violent crime is rife and Newark in 1971 and 1972 had the highest incidence of venereal disease in the nation. Housing in Newark was the worst in thirty cities surveyed by a nonprofit organization consisting of lawyers, economists, and others. It received very low marks in five separate categories: cost, crowding, plumbing, segregation of housing, and racial discrimination in rentals. "Newark's housing is sick,'' Mayor Gibson has confessed.[25] While Gibson himself is not at fault, he has not been able to better the situation.

The same point can be made about Richard Hatcher who was elected mayor of Gary, Indiana, in 1967. Until Hatcher's election, Afro-Americans rarely took an active part in the political life of the city which had been a creature of the gargantuan United States Steel Corporation. Hatcher's accomplishments should not be minimized. He has energetically enforced housing codes. He has regularized garbage collection, theretofore an erratic process in black neighborhoods.[26] But, despite his undoubted ability and honesty, despite the infusion of federal funds into Gary, Hatcher has not appreciably ameliorated the lot of the average black.

Clearly, black success at the urban polls will not usher in the millennium. Unchanged and seemingly unchangeable economic realities are powerful constraints on the potential good that can come from the political process. Naturally this is not an argument against black citizens making maximum use of their constitutional rights. It is an argument against politically motivated fertility. The thesis that black political domination of the cities will collectively move black Americans a giant step toward Utopia is dubious at best. Even if the opposite were true, indiscriminate unplanned breeding surely creates more individual suffering than it can possibly relieve. And from the moral point of view, producing children to be electoral units is no more justifiable than begetting them to be military cannon fodder.

Census data in 1970 disclosed that there are one hundred and two counties, all in the South, that are at least half black. Taken in conjunction with the voting rights which blacks increasingly exercise, these statistics point to a tremendous new political potential. Afro-Americans in Dixie are already electing public officials of their race at a rate unparalleled since Reconstruction. In 1965 only seventy-two blacks held elective office in the South. Nine years later that figure had jumped to 1,307, an increase of 1800 percent. This astounding change was not a result of a rise in black residents in the old slave states. Rather it was made possible by the Voting Rights Act of 1965.[27] Voter education and voter registration compaigns among traditionally powerless blacks have obviously yielded dramatic political results. If the one man one vote concept is fully realized, blacks are bound to further augment their political strength. But the lesson to be learned from success at the polls is that political potential can and should be exploited for the benefit of the black community by having every eligible voter exercise the franchise. The lesson to be learned is not that political power flows from production-line reproduction. For black Americans such as the late Dr. Martin Luther King, Jr., the latter would be an exorbitant price to pay. He once stated that Negroes "do not wish for domination purchased at a cost of human misery. Negroes were once bred by slave owners to be sold as merchandise. They do not welcome any solution which involves population breeding as a weapon."[28] Dr. King, who had been catapulted into national prominence by his role in the Montgomery bus boycott in 1955, richly deserved the Nobel Peace Prize bestowed on him. As a champion of humanitarianism he had few equals. Procreation that was prompted by political dogma could not be reconciled with that humanitarianism.

The "strength in numbers" school of thought has been assailed on tactical as well as moral grounds and not only by so-called moderates. Julius Lester is an accomplished musician, a writer, and a teacher. At one time he was also a field secretary for the Student Nonviolent Coordinating Committee (SNCC). Lester believes that black revolutionaries should urge their women to postpone having children so that they may fully participate in the battle. "There is power in numbers," he has conceded "but that power is greatly diminished if a lot of those numbers have to sit at home and change diapers instead of being on the front lines, where most of them would rather be."[29]

## NOTES

1. Victor DuBois, *Population Review 1970: Ivory Coast,* American Universities Field Staff Reports, West Africa Series XIII, No. 1 (1971): 11-12.

2. J. Mayone Stycos, "Public and Private Opinion on Population and Family Planning," *Studies in Family Planning,* No. 51 (March 1970): 14.

3. James R. Hooker, *Population Review 1970: Malawi,* American Universities Field Staff Reports, Central and Southern Africa Series XV, No. 1 (1971).

4. "International Planned Parenthood Federation: Survey of Member Organizations," *Studies in Family Planning,* No. 17 (February 1967): 14.

5. *Newsweek,* 12 June 1972.

6. Peter Dodds, director of the Family Planning Association of Rhodesia, letter to the author, 28 March 1974.

7. James R. Hooker, *Population Planning in Rhodesia 1971,* American Universities Field Staff Reports, Central and Southern Africa Series XV, No. 6 (1971): 2.

8. Mrs. J. C. Williams, national secretary of the Family Planning Association of South Africa, letter to the author, 1 May 1974.

9. Carl J. Stratmann, information officer of the Jamaica Family Planning Association Ltd., letter to the author, 13 December 1973.

10. Leonard E. Barrett, *The Rastafarians—A Study in Messianic Cultism in Jamaica* (Rio Piedras: Institute of Caribbean Studies, 1968), p. 51.

11. *The* [Kingston, Jamaica] *Star,* 8 February 1968.

12. *Advocate-News* [Barbados], 7 September 1972.

13. Ibid., 5 September 1972, and 7 May 1973.

14. Colonel O. F. C. Walcott, president of the Barbados Family Planning Association, personal interview, 4 April 1973.

15. *Advocate-News* [Barbados], 9 January 1973.

16. *Overseas Express* [Trinidad], 17 September 1973.

17. National Joint Action Committee, *The Black Woman—A Handbook* (n.p., March 1974), pp. 24-25.

18. Daniel H. Watts, "Birth Control," *Liberator,* May 1969, p. 3.

19. Roy Innis, personal interview, 17 May 1972.

20. Memo Wylda B. Cowles to Alan F. Guttmacher, president of

Planned Parenthood, 28 March 1966, re: Meeting with EROS in Berkeley, California on 23 February 1966.

21. Mary Smith, "Birth Control and the Negro Woman," *Ebony,* March 1968, pp. 28 ff.

22. United States Department of Commerce *News,* 11 January 1974.

23. Ibid., 25 April 1973.

24. Robert Curvin, "Black Power in City Hall," *Society,* September/October 1972, pp. 55-58.

25. *New York Times,* 12 November 1973.

26. Edward Greer, "The 'Liberation' of Gary, Indiana," *Transaction,* 8, No. 3 (January 1971): 30-39, 63.

27. *New York Times,* 1 March 1974.

28. Martin Luther King, Jr., *Family Planning—A Special and Urgent Concern* (New York: Planned Parenthood—World Population, n.d.), p. 5.

29. Julius Lester, "Birth Control and Blacks", in *Revolutionary Notes* (New York: Richard W. Baron, 1969), pp. 140-143.

# 7 . *Black Panthers,*
# *Black Muslims,*
# *Black Power*

"My Answer to Genocide," an *Ebony* cover story by Dick Gregory, is probably the best known single article on the subject of birth control and blacks.[1] Quite simply, Gregory's answer was "eight black kids—and another baby on the way." Gregory, a vegetarian, explained that birth control was contrary to nature. Therefore he could never use it.

But the principal point that emerges from the essay is that Gregory is mistrustful of any white-devised policy for blacks.

> For years they told us where to sit, where to eat, and where to live. Now they want to dictate our bedroom habits. First the white man tells me to sit in the back of the bus. Now it looks like he wants me to sleep under the bed. Back in the days of slavery, black folks couldn't grow kids fast enough for white folks to harvest. Now that we've got a little taste of power, white folks want us to call a moratorium on having children.[2]

Gregory blurred the distinction between the concept of family planning and the ideal of the small family. Furthermore, he grossly distorted the latter by suggesting that it meant no child-bearing at all. Perhaps most important of all Gregory seems to have said that nothing of value to blacks could come from the white power structure.

*Ebony*'s offices were deluged with correspondence in response to Gregory's article. Letters to the editor were published in subsequent issues. There was some backing for Gregory. However, the majority of letter writers, white and black, took issue with him. Many observed that the comedian was in a financial position to support his brood while a large family was disastrously burdensome for the average black. Other critics wrote that Gregory would have served his race better by adopting unwanted black children rather than having more of his own. *Ebony* itself apparently supported Gregory and his wife, Lillian. Mrs. Gregory won accolades in the "Backstage" feature of the December 1971 issue: "Maybe what black men really need is many more black women like Lillian Gregory."

Actually, Gregory's cynicism about birth control was not born with the *Ebony* article. He had previously questioned America's demographic policy in connection with our Vietnam misadventure. As a peace candidate for president of the United States in 1968, Gregory charged that this government stopped shipping pharmaceutical supplies to South Vietnam in 1967. Vietnamese civilians desperately needed drugs but contraceptives were the sole exception to the pharmaceutical export ban. "Evidently," Gregory surmised, "that commodity fits well with AID's anti-life bias which will deprive an underdeveloped people of lifesaving drugs."[3] Why the American government would withhold badly needed medicines from an ally is not made clear.

H. Rap Brown has also subscribed to the theory that governmental birth control programs designed for indigents are an attempt at genocide. Born in Baton Rouge, Louisiana, Brown attended traditionally black Southern University for a time. He subsequently enlisted in the Student Nonviolent Coordinating Committee and in 1967 succeeded Stokely Carmichael as chairman of that organization. A redoubtable figure in his black beret and sunglasses, Brown has never hidden the intense distaste he harbors for the land of his birth. He has referred to the United States as the "Fourth Reich" and the "world's slop jar."[4]

Brown became a fugitive from justice when he did not appear in a Maryland courtroom in April 1970 to stand trial on charges of inciting to riot and arson. The charges had grown out of an uprising that took place in Cambridge, Maryland, a few years earlier. In October 1971 Brown, who had long insisted that violence is "as American as cherry pie," was wounded and apprehended in an attempted holdup of a Manhattan bar. He was convicted and is currently serving a five- to fifteen-year prison term in New York State.

In his *Die Nigger Die* Brown gave a straightforward testament of the philosophy of doing and believing the opposite of whites. "If the white folks say it's more cultured to whisper, you talk loud. If white folks say gray suits are fashionable, you go buy a pink one." Brown has written that even as a teenager he "knew white folks couldn't do wrong right, so whatever they thought was good, I knew wasn't."[5] Whatever the enemy opposed deserved support. Whatever he supported merited opposition. Given the melancholy history of white subjugation of blacks in American history this attitude, while self-defeating, is not difficult to fathom. Still it overlooks the fact that even if a minority, or for that matter a majority, of whites foster black family planning for base motives, it may still be in the best interests of blacks to accept family planning.

In a sense the success of the birth control movement may militate against its acceptance by blacks whose alienation from the United States is almost total. It may be said that although there is still some opposition, birth control has been accepted, albeit grudgingly, by the Establishment and consequently anti-Establishment forces will be skeptical about it. The greater that acceptance is, the more available the contraceptive service, the deeper the skepticism will be, especially when other needs of the black poor are ignored. Thus, an anonymous black nationalist at Indiana University noted that abortions were free but aspirin cost money.[6] When Congress is remiss in its responsibility to rid the ghetto of rats, when it ignores the existence of malnutrition and the extraordinary danger hypertension poses to black Americans, when it fails to deal with the grave problem of lead poisoning among black slum dwellers, positive congressional action on family planning is bound to raise many black eyebrows.

Family planning is rarely seen in isolation from the black American dilemma, past and present. The Black Panther party newspaper views planned parenthood, black participation in the Vietnam War, venereal disease, and prostitution as part of the same picture. Coercive sterilization bills and restrictive welfare legislation are in the picture. So are inhuman living conditions, "police murders," rat bites, frequent fires, and accidents brought about by dilapidated houses. Together these constitute a malicious plan of genocide of black people concocted by the United States government. Additional evidence of the plan cited by the Panthers has been the reluctance of the government to institute a meaningful program of diagnosis, prevention, and treatment of sickle cell anemia. The United States was capable of sending men to the moon and it was scientifically able to cure other diseases, the Panther newspaper observed bitterly, but it "has refused to research or *disclose* [emphasis mine] the cure for a disease, practically all of whose victims are Black People." [7]

The Panthers have also invoked the "strength in numbers" argument. In 1970 when New York State liberalized its abortion law, the move was lambasted in the Black Panther organ: "Black people know that part of our revolutionary strength lies in the fact that we outnumber the pigs—and the pigs realize this too. This is why they are trying to eliminate as many people as possible before they reach their inevitable doom." [8]

Brenda Hyson, one of the female Panthers sharply critical of birth control, saw passage of the new law as a victory of an "oppressive ruling class who will use this law to kill off Blacks and other oppressed people before they are born." It was just a matter of time, she wrote, before voluntary abortion led to involuntary abortion and compulsory sterilization. She predicted that black women would shun "legalized murder" as they had "rejected the attempt to force family planning in the guise of pills and coils."[9]

Contrary to popular opinion, the Black Panthers are self-described Marxist revolutionaries, not black nationalists. In fact, they have often crossed swords figuratively and literally with cultural black nationalists such as the Los Angeles-based US organization. Eldridge Cleaver, the most celebrated Panther, is understood to have said that it is far more important for a black man to read Marx than to learn Swahili. Still, the Panthers seem to have viewed population matters through a black prism rather than a Marxist one.

Among black Americans, Marxist revolutionaries have not spearheaded the assault on family planning. While not every black nationalist espouses the genocide philosophy, the most caustic criticism of birth control comes from black nationalist sources. A rejection of birth control programs as genocidal was embodied in a resolution passed at the first national conference on black power held in Newark in 1967. A resolution introduced at a conclave held in Atlanta in September 1970 and billed as the "first modern pan-African Congress" lashed out at the United States for instituting programs of genocide in black communities by means of murder, drugs, the draft, abortion, and birth control.[10]

Epitomizing the black nationalist point of view was a strongly worded article in *Black News*, a youth-oriented biweekly published in Brooklyn. It excoriated the white man and charged him with perpetrating "deceptive genocide" by means of birth control. The "beast with an evil intellect" wanted to create a "blond-haired, blue-eyed world." To that end black women were duped into having unnecessary hysterectomies and surgical sterilization. The use of birth control pills and other contraceptives was vigorously disapproved by *Black News*. Of the condom it was said, "the hidden meaning of the Trojan was to emasculate the black man by convincing him that he should throw away his living sperm in the white man's rubber contraption rather than to put it into his woman's fertile womb."[11]

No black separatist organization has been more vitriolic in its condemnation of population control and family planning than the Nation of Islam, or the Black Muslims as they are popularly known. Scholars have traced this fascinating movement to one Noble Drew Ali, the founder in 1913 of a Moorish-American Science Temple in Newark. Ali claimed that Morocco was the original homeland of the black Americans, hence they were really Moors.[12] Upon his mysterious death the Islamic prophet was succeeded by W. D. Fard. Fard's background is murky, but black sociologist C. Eric Lincoln has written that when he arrived in Detroit in 1930 the black community believed him to be an Arab.[13] According to one legend, Fard was actually a Palestinian. Another had it that his father had been a Syrian of the Islamic faith.[14] A third listed his place of birth as the holy city of Mecca.[15] Black Muslims believe that Fard was the living embodiment of God, the long-awaited messiah of the Christians, the "Mahdi" of the Muslims. After Fard's strange disappearance in 1934, Georgia-born Robert Poole became leader of the Nation of Islam, the black nationalist sect which he fashioned and nurtured until his death in February 1975. Poole was Elijah Muhammad.

In common with Muslims the world over, followers of Elijah Muhammad are strict monotheists. For them there is but one God and Allah is his name. Facing in the direction of Mecca they pray five times a day as do observant Muslims everywhere. They observe the holy month of Ramadan. But they ignore the lunar calendar which determines the annual observance for Muslims elsewhere and celebrate it instead in December. Certain food taboos are also shared, e.g., black Muslims abstain from eating pork.

Devotees of Elijah Muhammad feel that integration of the races is a snare and a delusion. They want complete separation in a state or territory of their own. They have purchased some farmland in the South. At the same time they have been striving for economic self-determination in urban areas where Muslims operate restaurants, groceries, apartment houses, and other businesses. Because they wish to insure that their children will be taught and trained by their own teachers, the Muslims maintain their own schools.

Adherence to the Black Muslim code of conduct can mean an austere regimen. Abstinence from the use of tobacco and alcohol is required. Overeating is frowned upon and corpulence may elicit a fine from the Muslims. Gambling and profanity are sinful.

White women are viewed as satanic temptations to black men and the Black Muslim program favors the legal prohibition of intermarriage or race mixing. Even among themselves there is a puritanical quality to much Black Muslim thinking. Divorce is permitted but disapproved of by the Muslims. Philandering is a punishable offense. One Muslim minister has endorsed the rhythm system to prevent conception, but has denounced the pill as "just another convenience so man can play without pay." Contraceptives, minister Philbert Omar pontificated in 1970, destroy the moral fiber of a people.[16]

In August 1973 the American Bar Association was scored for a series of resolutions it had passed at its annual convention. Hardly a radical body, the American Bar Association had offended the Muslims by asking for the repeal of state laws which prevented minors from receiving contraceptive information and devices without parental approval; it called for the removal from statute books of all laws governing sexual activities involving consenting adults and laws which restricted voluntary contraceptive sterilization. In the Muslim view these and other resolutions regarding prostitution, the sale of pornography, and the use of marijuana were "designed to soften up . . . America for an onslaught of permissiveness and debauchery." There was fear that there would be "wholesale encroachment upon the mores and morality of the Black community."[17]

The Black Muslims' adamant opposition to birth control cannot simply be explained as prudishness and asceticism. It goes far beyond that and has much more to do with Muslim concern about the possible liquidation of blacks by "white devils."

The fear that birth control is a "death plan" was starkly expressed by Elijah Muhammad, prophet of the Chicago-based movement. In his book, *Message to the Blackman in America*, Muhammad admonished fellow blacks to be aware of the "tricks the devils [whites] are using to instill the idea of a false birth control in their clinics and hospitals." Blacks are further warned "of being trapped into the kind of disgraceful birth control laws now aimed exclusively at poor, helpless black peoples who have no one to rely on." Muhammad argued that the teachings of both the Bible and Holy Koran are against contraception. The white man's motive in supporting planned parenthood is seen not as that of promoting the well-being of Negro families, but of exterminating those families in the future. Muhammad actually saw a parallel between birth control and Pharoah attempting to destroy ancient Israel by murdering male Hebrew infants. Although such an analogy seems unbelievably simplistic, even paranoid, he cited as supporting evidence the example of a clinic in Fauquier County, Virginia, where impoverished black women were "pressured into accepting sterilizing."[18]

Birth control, it should be remembered, plays a crucial role in the central myth underlying the Black Muslim racial ideology. The original race was black, the Muslims say. The Caucasian race came into being when an apostate black scientist Yakub (sometimes spelled Yacub) made use of a rigid birth control law to kill off all the black babies on the mythical island of Pelan. Two millennia before Moses, Yakub embarked on his vile plan to murder black infants and replace them with white infants. And he was successful. After six hundred years, Malcolm X once asserted, "all they had left was a pale-skinned, blue-eyed, blond-haired thing you call a man. But actually the Bible calls him the devil."[19] Therefore, as Elijah Muhammad has written, Yakub, who lived to the ripe old age of one hundred and fifty, was both the father of the devil and author of the birth control law. To the Black Muslim seer it was transparent that the United States today is aiming at Yakub's same genocidal goal through the use of the contraceptive pill.[20] The pill is nothing less than a "bold offer of death," a weapon to enable the Caucasian race to rule the Negroid people who are the earth's rightful owners.[21]

Until his assassination in February 1965, no single Black Muslim was in the public eye more than Malcolm X. Born in Omaha in 1925, Malcolm was the son of a Baptist minister who worked as an organizer for Marcus Garvey's UNIA and who was slain by white racist vigilantes. Malcolm's turbulent life led him into underworld crime. He was a burglar, a narcotics peddler, and a procurer. The Muslims were his saviors. While in prison he was converted to Elijah Muhammad's faith and soon emerged as the most articulate Muslim spokesman. He remained a loyal disciple of Elijah Muhammad's until their falling out in 1964. Since his death in 1965 Malcolm has been virtually canonized by black Americans. A decade later he is one of the brightest stars in the black firmament.

Malcolm's opinions on planned parenthood were more complex than those ordinarily communicated by the Muslims. In a 1962 interview Malcolm expressed a preference for the term *family planning*. The phrase *birth control* was distasteful to him and he opined that "people, particularly Negroes, would be more willing to plan than to be controlled." Malcolm informed the interviewers, black field consultants for the Planned Parenthood Federation, that Black Muslim dogma did not proscribe family planning. He implied that techniques requiring discipline, e.g., the rhythm method or coitus interruptus, were used. It was apparent to the interviewers that Malcolm favored the use of planned parenthood services for health and economic reasons. However, mention of overpopulation elicited questions from him about why major efforts to control population growth were directed toward colored nations.[22] Malcolm indicated that he would be willing to cooperate in any way and he did arrange contact between Black Muslim women leaders and Planned Parenthood. For a time two women even attended sessions at Planned Parenthood clinics.

Before the interview with Malcolm, *Muhammad Speaks* had begun what could be interpreted as an anti-family planning campaign. Indeed, the interview was arranged so that Malcolm could be given a correct picture of birth control programs. Planned

Parenthood officials hoped to correct whatever misconceptions already existed. In the final analysis they were conspicuously unsuccessful.

In the following years the Muslims took an inflexibly hostile position. Birth control became an obsession. *Muhammad Speaks*, the widely read Black Muslim weekly, has published countless pieces, many of them front-page stories, decrying the "deadly nature and diabolic intentions behind birth control schemes."[23] Family planning has been seen as an integral element in a pattern of white oppression of blacks. A 1969 article in *Muhammad Speaks* alerted its readers to the "fact that, in this country, they are birth control targets far out of proportion to their percentage of the population—just like the Black soldiers in Vietnam are drafted, wounded and killed far out of their proportion in the population."[24] Coupling the population question with the debacle in Southeast Asia was another *Muhammad Speaks* article which said that the government was using birth control to hide the waste of the taxpayers' money on "criminal, supremacist profiteering warfare in Vietnam."[25]

Muslims do not see birth control as a compartmentalized issue isolated from the past maltreatment of blacks. Nor is it divorced from the myriad grievances, many quite legitimate, which they currently nurse against white American society. Family planning information and devices are more and more readily available to ghetto blacks. Why, the Muslims ask, is this the case when the same blacks are denied equal educational and job opportunities, fair wages, sufficient food, decent housing, and adequate health protection? [26] They often make the point that it is much simpler to obtain information about birth control than "true health necessities." Nothing else they require is theirs for the asking. Free medicine is not dispensed to jobless individuals or to the working poor. Yet black mothers who give birth in Cook County, Illinois, for example, are given, without charge, a two-month supply of contraceptive pills. When they are used up, clinics will provide more.[27]

It is undeniably true that governments—national, state, and city alike—have been derelict in their duty toward black people. It is also true that government support for family planning among the poor has been given stingily and often for other than the humanitarian reasons preached by the unjustly maligned Planned Parenthood. Elected officials are eager to placate taxpayers who are infuriated by spiraling welfare costs. Family planning is appealing to the overburdened taxpayer because it offers the prospect of scaling down a monumental problem and saving him money. Because it smacks more of prevention than of cure, it is all the more appealing. But regardless of motivation, family planning works to the advantage of the black community as it redounds to the benefit of all communities. It means having babies by choice rather than by chance. For that reason alone it deserves the spirited support of all thinking persons. Even the Muslims have conceded that families should have the right to plan their size. In fact, in an unguarded moment several years ago Elijah Muhammad wrote that birth control was among the things free people had to know about to protect, preserve, and advance themselves.[28]

But, in general, the Muslims, infuriated by the damage wrought by racial bigotry, take a narrow, single-dimensional view of family planning. Existing birth control programs have to be crushed because they tell black people that "their economic and political problems—exploitation and racism—are really biological ones—fertility and love of children."[29]

In point of fact they do no such thing. In no way does planned parenthood deny that exploitation and racism have brought about the pits of despair which are our ghettos today. What it does is offer a *partial* solution to the manifold problems of the black poor. What it does is furnish individuals with the means necessary to plan the size of their family units and to space their children as they see fit, means heretofore withheld from them. It gives them the opportunity to maximize their potential as human beings and to harness and pool their resources. In doing so it puts them in a better position from which to launch a frontal attack on the twin evils of exploitation and racism.

Obviously, the Muslims, alienated as they are from white

America, have a completely different angle of vision. They contend that the "alarm and feverish attention now given to the 'population explosion' has long been one of the key 'alternatives' agreed upon by white world powers for preserving white supremacy."[30] For the Muslims the population crisis is unreal. Panic about overpopulation is a smokescreen for genocide. Famine can easily be averted by synthesizing nutrients and increasing the production of staple crops. With obvious relish *Muhammad Speaks* quoted a "Russian scientist" to buttress this point and blithely concluded that if the methods of producing and distributing food were altered hundreds of billions of people could be adequately fed.[31]

A 1970 article entitled the "Many Faces of Genocide" recalled that overt genocide against Africans began with the trans-Atlantic slave trade four hundred years ago. Population control, a white neo-Malthusian plot, was nothing more or less than genocide in a more sophisticated and subtle form.[32]

Cartoons in *Muhammad Speaks* have graphically conveyed the Muslim antipathy to birth control. For instance, one drawing, which was juxtaposed with a criticism of the Ford Foundation for its backing of fertility research, portrayed a cemetery with open graves each containing the body of a black infant. Inscribed on the grave markers were "scientist," "doctor," "lawyer," "teacher," "engineer," "inventor," suggesting the future professional attainments of the dead babies. A black woman standing at the gravesite holding a box of birth control pills [the box marked with a skull and crossbones] is thinking "Death For My Babies . . . And Race." A white gravedigger's comment is "Birth Control (Death) . . . Now There Will Be No More Negroes and Indians."[33]

In the same vein was a cartoon showing a white physician handing pills to a black woman. The woman is staring into a roaring furnace on which there is a sign reading "Birth Control—Death of A Nation." The caption reads, "Kill the Black Babies and Save the White—Orders by the Father (Yakub) To the White Race—Kill-Kill-Kill."[34]

Another cartoon accompanied a lengthy *Muhammad Speaks*

story entitled "How to Brainwash Women into Swallowing the Pill," based on the putative revelations of an unnamed black official of the Office of Economic Opportunity. The drawing depicted a black woman in an advanced state of pregnancy standing in a jail cell. She is explaining to fellow black prisoners the reason for her incarceration. The caption reads, "My Only Crime Was Refusing To Take Birth Control Pills."[35]

A cartoon published in 1973 shows four black women seated in a birth control clinic. Hooded, white-sheeted, pistol-wielding members of the Ku Klux Klan are trying to force their way into the waiting room of the clinic. But they are reproved by a white employee with these words: "Will You Guys Ever Learn There's More Than One Way To Skin A Cat."[36]

*Muhammad Speaks* in 1969 fretted over a reported decline in the black birth rate. The "powerful potential" held out by a growing black community was being threatened. As might be expected, Black Muslims believe that there is strength in numbers and they are persuaded that the white enemy believes the same thing. A black majority is not even necessary. White supremacists push population control, the Muslims have said, not because they are convinced that the black man is inferior but for the opposite reason—because he is clearly superior. So much so, in fact, that "he will rule this country if he reaches a 20 percent level of population."[37]

In October 1969 Lonnie Kashif of *Muhammad Speaks'* Washington bureau announced that the "demonic advocates of 'population controls' had escalated their war against the nonwhite people." Sterilization and abortion were two new lethal weapons in the white genocidal arsenal. The Association for Voluntary Sterilization was explicitly accused of exploiting the poor under the pretext of humanitarianism. The association's long opposition to coercive sterilization was overlooked. Instead, Kashif spoke of the association's "ungodly propaganda tactics," the "death of youth and denial of life."[38]

Abortion reform has often drawn the wrath of *Muhammad Speaks*. Columnist Lonnie Kashif saw the attempt to relax archaic anti-abortion laws as an escalation of the vicious attack on black motherhood. It was a "sinister spike of the multi-pronged war against all Black births."[39]

In January 1971 *Muhammad Speaks* reported on a pro-abortion women's march in Washington, D.C., during which one black feminist averred that, "Black women are uniting to control their own bodies. We will not be prone for you men any longer. We want the right to have abortions."[40] Other black females echoed her sentiments but *Muhammad Speaks* emphasized the infinitesimal black showing at the march. "Black Women Reject Abortions As Cure-all" was the title of the story.

Minister Louis Farrakhan, probably the Muslims' most dynamic spokesman since the defection of Malcolm X, has written that, "When the Black woman kills her unborn child, she is murdering the advancement of her nation." He has stated confidently that there is sufficient food on earth to feed mankind.[41]

Shirley Hazziez has written that Pharaoh's bid to exterminate the Israelites was child's play compared with the devil's efforts to destroy black babies with birth control pills and drugs. Miss Hazziez assured her readers that Allah was able to feed and care for black infants. She appealed to the black woman to decline the pill, "a deadly poison," and to rebuff the white enemy that advised blacks to decrease their numbers.[42]

Women occupy a subordinate position in the Nation of Islam. They know their place and are expected to play the traditional, dependent role of wife and mother. "The woman is man's field to produce his nation," Elijah Muhammad once wrote.[43] She is to be protected and elevated but not emancipated, it seems. Women are expected to eschew cosmetics and to dress modestly. There are no mini-skirted or bra-less Black Muslim women. They have remained impervious to women's liberation. Actually, they function as support figures for Muslim men. Weakness is said by the Muslims to be a woman's true nature, strength a man's true nature. On those rare occasions when Black Muslim women do make public statements they do not challenge well-established dogma.

Beyond the Muslim pale, however, blacks on the distaff side are not quite so compliant.

Hostility to contraception has produced some strange alliances. By reason of their shared antipathy to birth control, militant blacks and conservative Catholics have found themselves allied at times. One case in point is a Msgr. Charles O. Rice of Pittsburgh who is against artificial contraception on theological grounds. In 1969 he was also persuaded that black people had become the prime target of the Planned Parenthood Federation.[44] At that time Planned Parenthood had a black national chairman, black board members, and a goodly number of black staff, including the director of public relations. This situation, a happy one for those who believe that black self-determination is a good thing, was a source of distress to the prelate. Had Planned Parenthood been lily-white that would have been adduced as evidence that outsiders were foisting family planning on blacks. Obviously, it was a matter of heads we win, tails you lose. And why should Planned Parenthood not have directed its attention to blacks, other oppressed minorities, and poor whites? Upper- and middle-class white women who can pay for private gynecological and obstetrical services are not in need of Planned Parenthood.

Writing in *The Pittsburgh Catholic*, Msgr. Rice said that black genocide was an exaggeration, but the term was justified nonetheless ''because it describes a campaign to reduce the natural fertility of America's non-white population.'' He was also uncertain about the upshot of black people being inculcated with the birth control dogma. Without clarifying his meaning, Msgr. Rice conjectured that black instability could be worsened, that black males could be further emasculated, and that many black females could become reluctant to breed. Fearing the worst he flagellated whites for tampering with basics they did not understand.

Delighted with Msgr. Rice's ideas, the Black Muslims gave them additional circulation in the black ghettos. *Muhammad Speaks* published a lengthy story summarizing the priest's column. It was provocatively titled ''Paid to Front for Black Genocide?—Birth Control Group Hires Negro Stooge 'Pushers'."[45]

The religious and "genocidal" objections to birth control had been joined previously. In 1959 the late John Cardinal O'Hara had stated publicly that Negroes and Catholics, two groups with high birth rates, were the real targets of family planning programs. In the mid-1960s there was a bitter fight in Pennsylvania over state financing of family planning services through the Welfare Department. At that time the Roman Catholic bishops of Pennsylvania campaigned against planned parenthood by taking full-page advertisements in sixty newspapers across the state. The bishops hinted strongly that genocide of Afro-Americans was the motive of the state: "it is widely, though covertly, stated by birth prevention proponents both in and out of government that a significant 'benefit' of these programs would be their supposedly resulting check upon the expanding Negro populations in our major cities."[46] Racist phrases and defamatory innuendo regarding limiting the number of undesirables and the perils of black "proliferation" frequently accompanied discussion of the benefits of birth prevention, the bishops stated. At the root of the prelates' indignation was a new policy adopted by the Pennsylvania Department of Public Welfare in December 1965 which permitted recipients of public assistance to be referred, if they wished, for voluntary family planning services and information. In some instances, where serious problems of family functioning existed because of the inability of parents to limit the number of children born to them in accordance with their own interests and the health and welfare of family members, caseworkers could initiate discussions of birth control. The Catholic bishops were worried that "rights of conscience" and the "right to be left alone" were placed in jeopardy by this policy.

Overwhelmingly, black clergymen in Pennsylvania welcomed the state plan to give birth control information to the underprivileged. Bishop John Douglas Bright, presiding bishop of the First Episcopal District of the African Methodist Episcopal Church, an independent black denomination, was typical. Children ought not be ushered into this world to "live in ignorance, poor health, undernourished and unwanted," said Bishop Bright. Birth control was also a safeguard for the health of women in his enlightened view.[47]

In September 1962 the Most Reverend Patrick A. O'Boyle, Archbishop of Washington, preached a sermon on "Sterilization and the Medically Indigent." Sterilization, even if elective, was morally reprehensible to the cardinal. Contraceptive sterilization was never permissible, even with the consent of the individual concerned. The Catholic divine implied that sterilization programs for the medically indigent had a special impact on black people, a negative impact to be sure. He said that impoverished people— black Americans for the most part—were being treated as second-class citizens, as imbeciles and morons, and as irresponsible infants. To ease the burden of their more privileged neighbors they were being encouraged to have a maximum of three offspring while affluent whites able to pay their own medical bills were not influenced to restrict their family size.[48]

Cardinal O'Boyle's appeal to poor blacks and whites to say "yes to life" was feeble and disingenuous. The essence of his appeal was not altruism but theological rigidity. Middle-class Americans exercised free choice in the matter of sterilization. This "evil" ran counter to the cardinal's religious beliefs; consequently, he wanted to deprive all, regardless of race and class, of the right to control their own fertility.

Msgr. Rice, Cardinal O'Hara, and Cardinal O'Boyle have all tried to advance their religiously based opposition to contraception, abortion, and sterilization by playing upon black fears of genocide. Largely, but not exclusively, Catholic in inspiration and membership, the Right to Life movement has used the same tactic in its unflagging campaign against legalized abortion. Black women are not likely to be deluded.

## NOTES

1. Dick Gregory, "My Answer to Genocide," *Ebony*, October 1971, pp. 66 ff.
2. Ibid., p. 66.

3. Dick Gregory, *Write Me In* (New York: Bantam Books, 1968), pp. 62-63.

4. H. Rap Brown, *Die Nigger Die* (New York: The Dial Press, 1969), p. 138.

5. Ibid., p. 55.

6. Samuel F. Yette, *The Choice: The Issue of Black Survival in America* (New York: G. P. Putnam's Sons, 1971), p. 244.

7. *The Black Panther*, 4 January 1969; 10 April 1971; 8 May 1971. A national sickle cell anemia control act was finally passed by Congress in May 1972.

8. Ibid., 4 July 1970.

9. Ibid. Individual Panthers have broken ranks on the issue of planned parenthood and have participated in a free condom distribution program in North Carolina. In September 1970 one of the demands put forward at the Black Panther party's Revolutionary People's Constitutional Convention was for "free abortion, sterilization and contraceptive devices for men and women." But there was no mention of this in the Black Panther newspaper and the demand was probably made by whites at the conclave. A sizable number of whites, members of women's groups, gay movements, and other radical organizations were participants.

10. Imamu Amiri Baraka (ed.), *African Congress—A Documentary of the First Modern Pan-African Congress* (New York: William Morrow, 1972), p. 419.

11. Brother Kahlil, "Eugenics, Birth Control and the Black Man," *Black News*, 14 January 1971, pp. 20-21.

12. E. U. Essien-Udom, *Black Nationalism: A Search for An Identity in America* (New York: Dell Publishing Co., 1964), p. 46.

13. C. Eric Lincoln, *The Black Muslims in America* (Boston: Beacon Press, 1963), p. 10.

14. Ibid., p. 12.

15. Essien-Udom, *Black Nationalism*, p. 35.

16. *Detroit Free Press*, 27 November 1970.

17. *Muhammad Speaks*, 24 August 1973.

18. Elijah Muhammad, *Message to the Blackman in America* (Chicago: Muhammad Mosque of Islam No. 2, 1965), pp. 64-65.

19. Malcolm X, *The End of White World Supremacy—Four Speeches*, ed. Benjamin Goodman (New York: Merlin House, Inc., 1971), p. 56. Also see C. Eric Lincoln, *The Black Muslims in America* (Boston: Beacon Press, 1963), pp. 76-77.

20. *Muhammad Speaks*, 16 July 1965.

21. Ibid., 9 July and 23 July, 1965.

22. Memo from Wylda B. Cowles to Dr. Alan F. Guttmacher, president of Planned Parenthood, re: Interview with Malcolm X, 29 May 1962.

23. *Muhammad Speaks*, 24 January 1969.

24. Ibid., 29 August 1969.

25. Ibid., 11 July 1969.

26. Ibid.

27. Ibid., 4 July 1969.

28. Ibid., 11 July 1969; Elijah Muhammad, *Message to the Blackman*, p. 40.

29. *Muhammad Speaks*, 11 July 1969.

30. Ibid., 23 May 1969.

31. Ibid., 5 December 1969.

32. Ibid., 20 November 1970.

33. Ibid., 24 January 1969.

34. Ibid., 11 October 1968.

35. Ibid., 29 August 1969.

36. Ibid., 13 July 1973.

37. Ibid., 26 December 1969.

38. Ibid., 31 May 1969.

39. Ibid., 26 December 1969.

40. Ibid., 3 January 1971.

41. Minister Louis Farrakhan, "The Black Woman," *Essence*, January 1972, p. 31.

42. *Muhammad Speaks*, 3 January 1971.

43. Elijah Muhammad, *Message to the Blackman*, p. 58.

44. *Pittsburgh Catholic*, 21 February 1969.

45. *Muhammad Speaks*, 14 March 1969.

46. *Philadelphia Inquirer*, 20 June 1966.

47. *Philadelphia Evening Bulletin*, 20 December 1965.

48. "Sterilization and the Medically Indigent," Sermon delivered in St. Matthew's Cathedral, Washington, D.C., 9 September 1962.

# 8 . Blacks on the Distaff Side

Women's liberation is essentially a white, middle-class phenomenon. As such it has posed some thorny questions for blacks. Would competition between the women's movement and the ongoing struggle for racial justice weaken the latter? Would black involvement in women's liberation divert much needed psychic and physical energy from the black movement? Would black female assertiveness at this juncture in history further emasculate the Afro-American male? Would it divide blacks on sexual lines just when black unity is deemed imperative? Conflicting answers have been forthcoming and women's liberation has not made very much headway in black communities. Black feminists are rarely in the spotlight of public attention but, in the last few years, black feminist organizations have come into existence. There is growing awareness that black women are subject to a double disadvantage on account of their race and gender. "Black women have suffered cruelly in this society from living the phenomenon of being black and female in a country that is both racist and sexist," observed Margaret Sloan, an editor of *Ms.* magazine and a founder, in 1973, of the National Black Feminist Organization. Ms. Sloan and her group will not allow the black liberationists to forget that "there can't be liberation for half a race." [1]

At the same time, black women know all too well that they must cope with even greater stresses than their white sisters. Their burdens, physical and emotional, are greater. Black females have been quick to recognize that family planning and lawful abortions can often ease those burdens.

Except for women in the Nation of Islam and the Black Panther party, black women, including self-styled revolutionaries and nationalists, have often defiantly claimed the right to exercise freedom of choice in the matter of their own fertility. Dara Abubakari (Virginia E. Y. Collins), a vice-president of the separatist Republic of New Africa, has been quoted as follows:

> Women must be free to choose what they want. They should be free to decide if and when they want children. Maybe in this phase of the game we feel that we don't need any children because we have to fight the liberation struggle. So we won't have any children. We have the right to say so. Men shouldn't tell us. [2]

Written along the same lines was a manifesto by a black women's liberation group in Mount Vernon, New York, signed by two welfare recipients, two housewives, a domestic, and others. The statement indicted black men for making black women the "real niggers in this society—oppressed by whites, male and female, and black man too." The essence of their case was that:

> Black women are being asked by militant black brothers, not to practice birth control because it's a form of Whitey's committing genocide on black people. Well, true enough, but it takes two to practice genocide and black women are able to decide for themselves, like poor people all over the world whether they will submit to genocide. For us birth control is the freedom to fight genocide of black women and children.
> . . . Having too many babies stops us from supporting our

children, teaching them the truth . . . and from fighting black
men who still want to use and exploit us.[3]

Black women are beginning to look out for their own best
interests, Carolyn Jones has written. Black men who preached
against abortion were nowhere to be found when child support was
necessary. Miss Jones has found that "young black women who
watched their own mothers and grandmothers struggle to raise a
family alone, are no longer willing to listen to the black man's cry
of genocide."[4]

Toni Cade, a black author, has written approvingly of her black
sisters whose rejoinder to the call to abandon family planning has
been, "What plans do you have for the care of me and the child?
Am I to persist in the role of Amazon workhorse and slave? How
do we break the cycle of child-abandonment—ADC [Aid to
Dependent Children]?" Rearing black warriors for the revolution
is a fine goal but Miss Cade has serious doubts about achieving that
goal by "dumping the pill. You don't prepare yourself for the
raising of super-people by making yourself vulnerable—chance
fertilization, chance support, chance tomorrow." *Inter alia*
preparation meant being in control of yourself. "The pill gives the
woman, as well as the man, some control. Simple as that."[5]

Particularly hard-hitting on the issue of blacks and birth control
was a 1970 commentary by Linda La Rue, then a graduate student
at Purdue University. Ms. La Rue, using the *Black Scholar* as her
forum, took to task those such as black sociologist Robert Staples
who believe that the woman's contribution to the black liberation
struggle is basically her womb which yields the revolutionary
warriors of tomorrow.[6] Deftly cutting through the rhetoric about
birth control and the white man's machinations, she asks pointedly, "How many potential revolutionary warriors stand abandoned
in orphanages?" In her judgment, "a five-year moratorium on
black births until every black baby in an American orphanage was
adopted by one or more black parents," would represent a truly
meaningful revolutionary act. Such an unprecedented deed would

have the merit of humanitarianism—giving every "black child . . . a home and not just a plot in some understaffed children's penal farm" —and it would also aid the black liberation struggle.[7]

Maxine Williams and Pamela Newman, two black members of the Young Socialist Alliance, are well aware of the pilot experimental birth control projects which used Puerto Rican women as subjects. Therefore, they have said that they understand why "Third World" women sometimes view birth control and abortion as genocide. However, they believe that the central issue is the right of women to control their own bodies. Women, not male supremacists, ought to determine for themselves whether to have children or not.[8]

Maxine Williams has also lashed out at the Nation of Islam and the Reverend Jesse Jackson, founder and head of PUSH, People United To Save Humanity, because of their repeated anti-abortion statements. Jackson had said that abortion leads to "moral emptiness and aloofness." A former aide to Martin Luther King, Jackson had once advanced the following non sequitur: "If you can have an abortion you can wipe out villages in Vietnam and walk past ghettos." Ms. Williams' opinion was that Jackson's views "degrade women to the role of breeders." She talked also of the numberless black women whose lives were sacrificed when they were relegated to the backstreet butcher abortionists. To Reverend Jackson's contention that abortion is genocidal, Ms. Williams replied that just the reverse is the case: anti-abortion laws are genocidal.[9]

Marsha Coleman, a member of the Black Women's Task Force of the Women's National Abortion Action Coalition, has chided *Muhammad Speaks* for its criticism of black participation in an abortion repeal demonstration. Writing in *The Militant*, a socialist newsweekly, Ms. Coleman saw no conflict between the movement to liberate blacks and the movement to give black women control over their bodies and their lives.[10] *Muhammad Speaks*, which had denounced forced sterilization in the past, should also be against forced motherhood. Both policies kept women, especially black women, "in their place." At the same time Ms. Coleman repudiated "population-control schemes" because they were "racist" and "sexist."

Frances M. Beal, who was New York coordinator of the Black Women's Liberation Committee of SNCC has characterized governmental promotion of birth control in America's black communities and in developing nonwhite regions of the world as "outright surgical genocide." She has castigated the establishment of "sterilization clinics" to purge blacks of their reproductive potential. She has condemned the alleged practice of pressuring welfare women to undergo sterilization. Somewhat paradoxically Ms. Beal has attacked stringent abortion laws as "another means of subjugation, and, indirectly, of outright murder." Wealthy white women are able to have safe abortions, but poor black women are at the mercy of unqualified underworld abortionists. Ms. Beal has further indicated that she is not against black women practicing birth control. Indeed, black females have the "right and responsibility to determine when it is *in the interest of the struggle to have children or not to have them and this right must not be relinquished to anyone.* It is also her right and responsibility to determine when it is in *her own best interest* to have children, how many she will have, and how far apart."[11] The theme commonly expressed by Ms. Beal and other black spokeswomen is the desirability of free choice which has been denied to nonwhites.

Some black spokeswomen have unequivocally disavowed the genocide interpretation. Shirley Chisholm, the indomitable congresswoman from Brooklyn, has been among the most passionate apostles of planned parenthood. She was honored in the summer of 1969 by United Planned Parenthood for her stalwart support of the movement. In December of that year Mrs. Chisholm gave spirited testimony on behalf of a bill to expand, improve, and better coordinate the family planning services and population activities of the federal government. She testified that in her own "Bedford-Stuyvesant community, black women are glad to get direction in the area of family planning. I know that thousands of black women have been maimed by botched abortions because they couldn't get the family planning help that white women get."

A tireless fighter for abortion reform, she further informed the United States Senate Committee that the people in Harlem and Bedford-Stuyvesant did not think that family planning was a brand of genocide. "I have had hundreds of black women come to me over the past 10 years because they wanted family planning."[12]

*Muhammad Speaks* reproached Congresswoman Chisholm for her pro-abortion posture, speculating that she had come under the "burgeoning influence of the obvious genocidal purveyors" in her political camp. Mrs. Chisholm was echoing the sentiments of women's liberation and abortion repeal elements. Those elements, the puritanical *Muhammad Speaks* noted, favored free love and the liberalization of restrictive sex laws, and generally condemned morals, modesty, and marriage.[13] Operating on the assumption that she had been elected by "militant black anti-genocide New Yorkers," the Muslims also surmised that the congresswoman was paying other private political debts.

Mrs. Chisholm, the honorary president of the National Abortion Rights Action League, has called the portrayal of legal abortion programs and family planning as genocide "male rhetoric for male ears. It falls flat to female listeners, and to thoughtful male ones." In her book, *Unbought and Unbossed,* she has argued that two or three wanted youngsters who will be loved and educated can contribute more to racial progress than any number of children who are ill-fed, ill-clothed, ill-housed, and neglected.[14] To Mrs. Chisholm racial pride and simple humanity reinforce this attitude which, in other words, restates DuBois' dictum about quality and quantity. As already indicated, Mrs. Chisholm is not a lone eloquent black female voice. There are many others.

Mary Treadwell is the black executive director of a D.C.-based organization which provides job training and other rehabilitative services to blacks in need. She is committed both to feminism and to racial justice. No conflict exists between the two causes. Indeed they are complementary.

Speaking in 1971 before the Supreme Court's landmark decision that abortion was a private matter between a woman and her physician, Ms. Treadwell raised her voice to protest male-imposed restrictions on a female's right to control her own body, to conceive when she so chooses, and to terminate a pregnancy if she so chooses.[15] With pitifully few exceptions legislators in the United States are Caucasian males. By and large they have been unwilling to pass laws making abortion lawful. These same men, Ms. Treadwell said, "have never been faced with a knitting needle or coat hanger . . . nor have they swallowed masses of quinine tablets or turpentine only to permanently endanger physical well being."

Racial inequality in the practice of abortion prior to legalization predestined countless black women to unnecessary premature deaths in the prime of life. Roughly half of the puerperal or maternity-related deaths among black Americans and Puerto Ricans in New York City in the 1960s were attributed to criminal abortions as compared with just a quarter of puerperal mortality for Caucasian women.[16]

Black women were unable to afford medically safe illegal abortions. At the same time they were unable to take advantage of the existing therapeutic abortion laws. Hospital statistics substantiate this crucial point. Of all therapeutic abortions performed in New York City for the period 1951 to 1962, well over 90 percent were performed on white females.[17]

Choice in the matter of abortions has always been the prerogative of persons of means. In the event that no qualified physician in her own locality was willing to perform an illegal operation, a wealthier woman had the option of traveling to a jurisdiction within the United States or overseas where she could be aborted under sanitary conditions by a skilled doctor.

In 1962 Sherri Finkbine, an Arizona housewife, a mother of four, and a local television personality, decided that she was unwilling to take the grave risk of giving birth to a terribly deformed thalidomide baby. Unable to obtain a therapeutic abortion in her Phoenix hospital, she flew to Scandinavia for the operation. Religious hysteria transformed her personal ordeal into an internationally celebrated case. Needless to say, Mrs. Finkbine's solution was not feasible for housewives in Harlem, Watts, or Roxbury.

Lacking the economic means, black and other minority women who wanted to end their pregnancies placed themselves in the hands of untrained backstreet abortionists. Their only alternative was an equally perilous self-induced abortion. There is no doubt that the poor—among them black, Puerto Rican, and other minority women—were the chief victims of the antiquated, restrictive abortion laws.

With the legalization of abortions, safer procedures have been made available to the indigent. Cost is no problem as Medicaid pays the bills. The director of maternity services and family planning for the Department of Health in New York City reports that it is now very unusual for black women to be admitted to city hospitals following bungled abortions.[18] Harlem Hospital's Department of Obstetrics and Gynecology reported 1,011 admissions for incomplete abortion in 1965. Seven years later, in 1972 that figure had dropped to 272, and in 1973 it was down to 199.[19] Black women are now seeking abortions for economic, health, and personal reasons. For the year ending June 30, 1973, black women residing in New York City had 47.6 percent of the abortions compared with 39 percent for white women, although there are two times as many white women of childbearing age.

Legalization of abortion has also reduced the illegitimacy rate among blacks (as it has among whites). After abortion became legal in California, the steady rise in illegitimate births was radically reversed. A review of two years of experience in New York City has shown that liberalized abortion had a similar impact on illegitimacy in that city. Even more significant in purely humanitarian terms is the conclusion of Pakter et al. that the availability of legal abortion to low-income women in New York City has led to a dramatic drop in maternal mortality associated with pregnancy termination and to a sharp decline in infant mortality.[20]

Black women are now determined to act instead of being acted upon, as was so often the case in the past. Their resolve is evident in the black feminists' opposition to an anti-abortion rider attached to a Medicaid bill by Senator James Buckley, the conservative Republican junior senator from New York. Senator Buckley's amendment would completely bar the use of Medicaid funds for abortions. Black spokeswomen saw the Buckley move as a threat to the dignity, the health, the very lives of women, especially poor black and brown women. Welfare recipients would be directly affected. In a strongly worded statement issued in December 1973 the black spokeswomen pointed out that the majority of women in New York City who had benefited from lawful abortions during the preceding three years had been black and Puerto Rican. They accused Senator Buckley of wanting to turn back the clock, of "condemning the nation's poor once more to the indignities and dangers they suffered in the bad old days—while those with private resources continue to get safe, legal abortions."[21]

Mary Treadwell has also skillfully demolished the genocide proposition: "There is no magic in a home where someone has reproduced five or more black babies and cannot manage economically, educationally, spiritually nor socially to see to it that these five black babies become five highly trained black minds." There was no dearth of black babies, she noted. Thousands were to be found in foster homes and in public institutions. Ms. Treadwell urged blacks to adopt black children and to help shape their futures. "Black people cannot afford pregnancy as an ego trip." [22]

Many black women concur. Across the country they have earnestly requested, even demanded, that fertility control facilities be put at their disposal. A Detroit ghetto affords an instructive case study. There the neighborhood women organized and persuaded the Mom and Tots Center, a storefront health enterprise, to provide various medical services. Birth control was of paramount concern. Mom and Tots happily accommodated them and the family planning caseload grew apace. On one occasion a male functionary from the Freedom Now party visited the center and began to sermonize about genocide. He trotted out the usual arguments—that the pills were unsafe, that experimentation involving pills had been done on poor folks, that birth control was a means employed by the white establishment to manipulate Afro-Americans. He was asked how people who used the services of the center could be pressured into doing what they were unwilling to do. After further discussion, he left somewhat chastened, his ideology punctured by a heavy dose of common sense.[23]

When Detroit was convulsed by a major black riot in the summer of 1967, buildings on both sides of the Mom and Tots Center were gutted, but the center remained standing. Amidst the burning and looting it survived virtually unscathed. A black activist told why. Black people were convinced of the goodness of the Mom and Tots personnel. "We know them and they know us. They work with us, not on us like one works on a machine or a piece of wood. They care for us. We know we can stop in and they'll help us when we ask them things. They ask us to make decisions on how to run the place. They treat us like first-class human beings because we are first class human beings. They have respect for us and we respect them."[24]

Either because of the genocide myth or out of a perverted sense of machismo, black men spoke out against the abortion clinic at Harlem Hospital when it was first opened. Nonetheless, black women went to the clinic to terminate their unwanted pregnancies and returned for family planning counseling. Around twenty thousand women now attend annually to learn about planning parenthood.[25]

On occasion black women have asserted themselves and clashed head-on with black men purveying the genocide philosophy. In Bedford-Stuyvesant early in 1966 an all-day seminar on planned parenthood was held for two hundred and fifty black women working as community aides in a youth program. A small number of black males and some fifteen, young, unmarried mothers also attended. Following presentations by a biracial panel of Planned Parenthood speakers, one of the black men in the audience asked questions such as "How come you people only have clinics in Negro neighborhoods?" and "Why are you trying to push this down our throats?'' A young mother then delivered an impassioned tirade arguing that it was the women who had to bear and care for their offspring and decisions about birth control were theirs to make. The women in the assemblage greeted her remarks with thunderous applause.[26]

Another collision occurred in Pittsburgh. In December 1967 the *New York Times* reported that local family planning clinics had been accused of taking action to keep the birth rate among blacks as low as possible and of operating "without moral responsibility to the black race." The accuser claimed that they had become an instrument of genocide. Dr. Charles Greenlee, a black Pittsburgh physician who made these charges, also complained about "pill-pushing" by inquisitive, untrained white workers in black neighborhoods.[27] Dr. Greenlee, who was identified with the NAACP in Pittsburgh, subsequently protested that those workers approached only black women in poverty areas.[28] The physician told the press that he was not opposed to planned parenthood as such. Rather he objected to programs sponsored by the Office of Economic Opportunity which allegedly concentrated family planning clinics in black neighborhoods. The motive, Dr. Greenlee declared, was "to make less niggers so they won't have to build houses for them."[29]

Greenlee's highly vocal ally was one William Bouie Haden, a former grocery store proprietor, who led a black organization called the United Movement for Progress. The pill, Haden cautioned his followers, could "lead to a bigger massacre of black people than the Germans' killing of the Jews."[30] Haden was incensed because the white political establishment was unwilling to appropriate money for rat control in the ghettos, but was ready to "spend thousands to make sure you can't have any babies."[31]

The mobile planned parenthood clinic in the black Homewood-Brushton area of Pittsburgh was closed as a result of the combined efforts of Greenlee and Haden. Afterwards, Haden warned that firebombings and rioting would result "if anyone tries to operate a birth control project in the area."[32] Seventy black women who wanted the clinic reopened protested but to no avail. In February

1969 five other poverty neighborhoods were denied funds for planned parenthood facilities mainly because of Haden's activities.

Again black women spearheaded the counterattack. The local branch of the Welfare Rights Organization, whose members were recipients of public assistance, was upset by the decision to eliminate clinics in their neighborhoods. The welfare mothers clarified their support for planned parenthood in a press release on 24 February 1969. They did not want to be told how many children to have. "We think a mother can better care for her family if she can control the number of children she bears, and we think that a mother deserves the opportunity to decide when her health and well-being is better served by preventing conception." Free choice was the crux of the dispute. The Welfare Rights Organization also observed that "most of the anti-birth control pressure is coming from *men!*—Men who do not have to bear the children. We're speaking for the women and we want the Planned Parenthood Centers to stay in our neighborhoods." As a consequence of agitation by a few hundred poor black women, the federal funds originally earmarked for birth control were restored in March of that year. Haden had been snubbed by the very people he had claimed to represent. Little has been heard from Haden or Greenlee since.

## NOTES

1. *New York Times*, 16 August 1973. Also see "Feminism: 'The Black Nuance,'" *Newsweek*, 17 December 1973, pp. 89-90.

2. Quoted in Gerda Lerner (ed.), *Black Women in White America—A Documentary History* (New York: Pantheon Books, 1972), p. 587.

3. Quoted in Robin Morgan (ed.), *Sisterhood Is Powerful—An Anthology of Writings from the Women's Liberation Movement* (New York: Vintage Books, 1970), pp. 360-361.

4. Carolyn Jones, "Abortion and Black Women," *Black America*, No. 5 (September 1970): 49.

5. Toni Cade, "The Pill: Genocide or Liberation," ed. Toni Cade, in

*The Black Woman: An Anthology* (New York: Signet Books, 1970), pp. 163-164.

6. Robert Staples, "The Myth of the Black Matriarchy." Reprinted from *The Black Scholar*, February 1970, p. 10.

7. Linda LaRue, "The Black Movement and Women's Liberation." Reprinted from *The Black Scholar*, May 1970, p. 8.

8. Maxine Williams and Pamela Newman, *Black Women's Liberation* (New York: Pathfinder Press, Inc., 1970), p. 9.

9. *The Militant*, 16 March 1973.

10. Marsha Coleman, "Are Abortions for Black Women Racist?" *The Militant*, 21 January 1972, p. 19.

11. Frances M. Beal, "Double Jeopardy: To Be Black and Female," ed. Robin Morgan, *Sisterhood Is Powerful*, pp. 340-353.

12. These quotations are from Richard Lincoln, "S 2108: Capitol Hill Debates the Future of Population and Family Planning," *Family Planning Perspectives* 2, No. 1 (January 1970): 6-12.

13. *Muhammad Speaks*, 26 December 1969.

14. Shirley Chisholm, *Unbought and Unbossed* (New York: Avon Books, 1971), pp. 127-136.

15. Mary Treadwell, "Is Abortion Black Genocide?" *Family Planning Perspectives* 4, No. 1 (January 1972): 4-5.

16. Robert E. Hall, "Abortion in American Hospitals," *American Journal of Public Health* 57, No. 11 (November 1967): 1933-1936. Also see Edwin M. Gold, Carl L. Erhardt, Harold Jacobziner, and Frieda Nelson, "Therapeutic Abortions in New York City: A 20-Year Review," *American Journal of Public Health* 55, No. 7 (July 1965): 964-972.

17. Gold et al., p. 966.

18. *New York Times*, 6 December 1973.

19. James A. Batts, director, Department of Obstetrics and Gynecology, Harlem Hospital Center, letter to the author, 8 August 1974.

20. June Sklar and Beth Berkov, "The Effects of Legal Abortion on Legitimate and Illegitimate Birth Rates: The California Experience," *Studies in Family Planning* 4, No. 11 (November 1973): 281-292; Jean Pakter, Donna O'Hare, Frieda Nelson, and Martin Svigar, "Two Years Experience in New York City with the Liberalized Abortion Law— Progress and Problems, *American Journal of Public Health* 63, No. 6 (June 1973): 524-535.

21. Statement quoted in the *Planned Parenthood—World Population Washington Memo*, 7 January 1974.

22. Treadwell, "Is Abortion Black Genocide?" p. 4.

23. Nancy Milio, *9226 Kercheval—The Storefront That Did Not Burn* (Ann Arbor: University of Michigan Press—Ann Arbor Paperback, 1971), pp. 84-85.

24. Ibid., p. 140, quoting from C. O'Brien, *The Detroit Free Press*, 30 July 1967.

25. *New York Times*, 6 December 1973.

26. Planned Parenthood Memo. Mrs. M. Manisoff to Mrs. Dorothy Millstone, 3 February 1966.

27. *New York Times*, 17 December 1967.

28. *Pittsburgh Press*, 21 August 1968.

29. *New York Post*, 7 October 1968.

30. *Pittsburgh Courier*, 24 August 1968.

31. *Pittsburgh Press*, 21 August 1968.

32. Ibid., 15 August 1968.

# 9 . *Reservations Among the Most Reasonable*

Dr. Charles Greenlee's position on birth control contrasts sharply with that of the oldest and largest of the civil rights organizations, the NAACP. At its fifty-seventh convention in 1966 considerations of family well-being prompted the NAACP to adopt a policy statement which said in part: "mindful of problems of family health and economic stability, we support the dissemination of information and materials concerning family health and family planning to all who desire it." Four years later an editorial in *The Crisis* talked of the population explosion, a phenomenon which required that greater attention be paid to family planning. "The future of the entire human race is at stake." It took note of the division within the black community over the issue of birth control and criticized those blacks who seemed to espouse the "Hitler doctrine of babies and more babies, regardless of the circumstances into which they were born or of the prospect of their attaining the good life." On the other hand, it pointed out that more babies were needed, and poor black people should not reject parenthood out of despair.[1] It did not elaborate on the need for more babies. To be sure, some members of the NAACP and some local branch activists do have reservations about birth control for blacks, but as recently as April 1972 John Morsell, the assistant executive director, wrote: "it is a fact that the national leadership of the NAACP believes in family planning as a social value and rejects the notion . . . that this is a form of genocide."[2]

The National Urban League, which like the NAACP is biracial, middle-class, and pro-integration, has endorsed family planning for more than thirty years. The league was established in 1911 to ease the adjustment of black migrants to urban life and to improve industrial conditions for Negroes in the cities. Concerned with strengthening family life and with reducing individual and family dependency, the league's Board of Trustees in 1962 came out unequivocally for "positive and realistic programs of family planning." All persons were entitled to know about the various methods of birth control and to choose among them consistent with their own value systems and religious convictions. At that time many welfare departments still refused to involve themselves in family planning, even as referral agencies. The Urban League charged that this practice undercut the effectiveness of programs to make welfare recipients self-supporting. It stated that, "To prohibit case workers in public welfare agencies from discussing family planning resources with their clients is a discrimination which denies to welfare recipients one of the principal means of family health and progress utilized by more affluent couples."[3] Whitney Young, the late executive director of the league, once wrote that the responsibility of tax-supported welfare and medical agencies to impart information about birth control was as basic as their obligation to share information about the availability of polio innoculations or X-rays.[4] Local officials of Urban League affiliates have also taken strong pro-family planning positions. For example, the Chicago Urban League has stated that "Birth Control is essential to the War on Poverty and that to fight poverty without birth control is to fight with one hand tied behind the back."[5]

The Urban League has not merely paid lip service to planned parenthood. A national director for family planning has been appointed to promote it actively. In addition, contraceptive services are being offered at league-operated clinics. Planned parenthood is an integral part of the agency's family life education program. One league poster directed at the distaff side showed a black woman wearing her hair in the Afro or natural state. The copy read "It's your show . . . don't mess with it. Get the facts on family planning."

The National Medical Association, the Negro counterpart of the American Medical Association, explicitly endorsed the provision of family planning services to those unable to pay for them in 1962. At its annual conference in 1968 the NMA, after noting the high infant and maternal mortality rates for blacks, recommended that more comprehensive health care programs be established to provide total medical care and include family planning.

However, it was also in 1968 that three black physicians associated with the Watts [Los Angeles] Extended Health and Family Planning Group Inc. declared their intention to "keep watchful vigil over the sanctity of procreation among black people." Alarmed by the rising tide of conservatism in the country, they were fearful that federally administered programs might be used to diminish the black population of America. They recognized the need for family planning, but they insisted that "it be offered in a dignified manner along with ancillary health services."[6]

In the 1960s and 1970s eminent black individuals who are usually categorized as moderate and anti-separatist have normally taken pro-birth control stances. In 1966, two years before his assassination, Martin Luther King was the recipient of the Margaret Sanger Award in Human Rights. In accepting the award, Dr. King remarked that

Negroes have no mere academic nor ordinary interest in family planning. They have a special and urgent concern. . . . The Negro constitutes half the poor of the nation. Like all poor, Negro and white, they have many unwanted children. This is a cruel evil they urgently need to control. There is scarcely anything more tragic in human life than a child who is not wanted.[7]

Carl Rowan, formerly United States ambassador to Finland and now a syndicated columnist, has written in favor of government involvement in birth control programs as a crucial aspect of medical care. The result of such involvement, Rowan says, would not be mass sterilization of Afro-Americans and other oppressed minorities. It would not be America's "final solution" to the nonwhite problems as some fear. "It is like saying that because government now supports medical care for the aged pretty soon Federal bureaucrats will decide who must have a gall bladder operation, or that old people must become the victims of euthanasia because keeping them alive is too costly."[8]

There are many other prominent black proponents of planned parenthood. Among them is James Farmer, national director of the Congress of Racial Equality when that organization was still integrationist in orientation and makeup. Appearing on the CBS-TV program "Face the Nation" on April 25, 1965, Farmer stated a need for family planning for blacks. At this time, CORE community centers in the North and in the South were running classes on family planning.

Bayard Rustin, chief organizer of the 1963 March on Washington, also boosts planned parenthood. Rustin a long-time trade unionist, sees conception limitation as a necessity for the poor, both black and white; otherwise they can never hope to move up the proverbial social and economic ladder. Overly large families, he has stated, are burdensome to the family members and to society at large. In a statement issued in March 1967, Rustin pointed out that it was imperative for the civil rights movement to enlarge its program so that the grass-roots poor would profit from family planning education and instruction.

Dr. Jerome H. Holland, a distinguished black sociologist and educator, served for a time as chairman of Planned Parenthood-World Population before becoming the United States ambassador to Sweden. Holland championed his agency's critically important decision to recognize abortion and sterilization as proper medical procedures. Those who called birth control genocide, he said, were "not aware of the real meaning of family planning and its use."

More than once, members of the Congressional Black Caucus have co-sponsored family planning legislation in the House of Representatives. Ron Dellums, a California Democrat, is a case in point. For his outspokenness on controversial issues Congressman Dellums has been called many unflattering names. But "Uncle Tom" is almost never among them. In January 1973 Dellums introduced a measure in the lower house to "promote public health and welfare by expanding and improving the family planning services and population research activities of the Federal Government."⁹ Dellums' bill made it clear that he was concerned that unwanted children were impairing the stability and adversely affecting the health and well-being of each individual in the family unit. He was troubled by the fact that, owing to their poverty, some six and a half million women in America were denied access to up-to-date, effective, medically safe, planned parenthood services. He understood that among the happy sequelae of family planning are a lowered maternal and infant mortality rate and a reduced incidence of premature births and sundry infant diseases. Alleviation of the privations of impoverished persons would also ensue. Dellums' bill stated that "family planning has been recognized nationally and internationally as a universal human right."¹⁰

Blacks who have been elected to Congress aim to guarantee that right for their racial brethren. Ms. Barbara Jordan, who represents a Texas constituency, has written that the theory that *voluntary* contraception, abortion, and sterilization are part of a genocidal conspiracy directed at Afro-Americans just won't wash.¹¹

But three and a half centuries of persecution have left a legacy of mistrust which affects the thinking of some of the most reasonable and responsible "moderate" blacks. That mistrust is often evident in their statements on population questions. For example, in a parley on the health needs of black Americans held in Nashville, Tennessee, in 1971 it was found that "blacks believe any national program which focuses on family planning is a desperation move on the part of whites to remain in control since they were not concerned about the family structure of blacks a century and a half ago.'' Unlike population control, which was unacceptable, family planning was acceptable to the conferees provided it was an integral part of a comprehensive health program. As matters stood, however, there was ''too much emphasis on the planning and not enough emphasis on the family.''[12]

This same mistrust was apparent in the comments of individuals of the stature of Julian Bond and the late Langston Hughes. The multi-talented Hughes wrote a column in 1965 on the ''Population Explosion'' in which his famous character, Simple said:

> White folks are not thinking about being sterilized, neither in war nor peace. It is India, China, Africa and Harlem they is considering—300 million dollars worth of birth control for us! You know I really do believe white folks has always got something up their sleeve for colored folks. Yes, they has.[13]

Five years later, the dynamic Georgia legislator, Julian Bond, addressing a Syracuse University commencement audience, suggested that the intense interest in the population explosion could lead to genocide of black Americans and other poor people. ''Without the proper perspective the *Population Bomb* becomes a theoretical hammer in the hands of the angry, frightened and powerful racists, as well as over the heads of black people, as the ultimate justification for genocide.'' He inferred that black Americans had good cause to be alarmed.[14]

The *Population Bomb* to which Julian Bond alluded was the title of a controversial book by a population biologist at Stanford University, Dr. Paul R. Ehrlich.[15] While presenting a frightening exposition of the population problem and its attendant dangers to mankind, the book also made an eloquent plea for stabilizing the world's population, for lowering the growth rate to zero, even ''making it go negative.'' Ehrlich is honorary president and past president of Zero Population Growth (ZPG), a national organization originally founded in California to educate the public in general and legislators in particular about the issue of overpopulation; to press for enactment of far-reaching birth control programs; and to promote research into population problems and more effective contraception. Most advocates of ZPG talk about arresting population growth by means of tax incentives not to reproduce beyond a certain limit, by legalizing abortion, and by making population education an integral part of school curricula. A minority within the organization profess a belief in the necessity of compulsory birth regulations.

Edgar Chasteen, a professor of sociology and board member of ZPG, warns that the stork is not the bird of paradise and declaims that "we have to rid ourselves of outmoded values concerning laissez-faire parenthood and establish sensible and compulsory limits to family size."[16] A few ZPG zealots favor adding sterilants to water supplies and staple foods. Not surprisingly, it is the extreme coercive techniques which receive the greatest publicity and give the movement to curb population growth an unfavorable image with certain blacks.

Dr. William Darity, chairman of the Public Health Department at the University of Massachusetts, has tartly called ZPG "genocide for our black people." At a Yale University debate in January 1972, he said that ZPG's emphasis on planned parenthood is designed to reduce and control the black population.[17]

"To many blacks the '0' sounds like zero black children," Naomi Gray told the Commission on Population Growth and the American Future.[18] Ms. Gray had worked for Planned Parenthood for eighteen years.

Eugene S. Callender, president of the New York Urban Coalition, submitted a statement to the Population Commission contending that oppressed minorities consumed only a small percentage of America's resources. Hence, he asked why blacks should countenance moves to limit their freedom so that white middle-class life-styles would not be threatened. Projections of overpopulation for the year 2000 did not frighten Callender, but he was afraid that "national policy will be so devised that we restrict freedom—freedom to choose and freedom to protest."[19]

This outlook is easily understood. Denizens of decaying slums can hardly be expected to respond with alarm to predictions that continued population growth will impair the quality of life in America. The quality of their lives is already impaired. Overcrowding is already a fact of everyday life to them. Beset by a multitude of race-related personal problems, they cannot realistically be expected to become emotionally preoccupied with the threatened extinction of the peregrine falcon even if it is the world's fastest bird and once served as the hunting companion of kings. Ghetto dwellers consider themselves an endangered species.

Minorities have not caused the ecological crisis, but, to the degree that overpopulation results in environmental deterioration, they are the main losers, ZPG leaders have argued persuasively. "Poor blacks are confined to the cores of cities where air pollution is heaviest and urban decay and overcrowding are worst. Black Americans . . . have significantly higher average levels of D.D.T. in their tissues . . . Chicanos . . . suffer directly from polluting agricultural practices, especially the misuse of pesticides."[20] Cribbed, cabined, and confined to the ghetto, black Americans do not need any reminder of their sardine-can predicament. A decade and a half ago the United States Civil Rights Commission advanced a thought-provoking hypothesis regarding the overcrowded living conditions of urban blacks: "If the population density in some of Harlem's worst blocks obtained in the rest of New York City, the entire population of the United States could fit into three of New York's boroughs."

ZPG has urged parents to stabilize American population growth by having no more than two children per family. Reverend Jesse Jackson, who until his resignation in December 1971 was director of Operation Bread-basket, the economic arm of the Southern

Christian Leadership Conference, has demurred. In an interview given in 1971, he said that everyone talks about controlling population but "nobody suggests that the Kennedy women stop having children because there's respect for their freedom to do whatever they want."[21] Jackson's implication is that population controllers reflect both class and race prejudices. But Paul Ehrlich has gone to great pains to demonstrate that the swelling of the American body politic is not due to the unrestrained multiplication of poor people. Affluent, middle-class couples are responsible for more than two-thirds of the newborn babies annually added to our population. Therefore, the latter should be the first target of any government effort to lower the birth rate. Simply put, Ehrlich's position is that "*any* couple with more than two children is contributing to the population explosion."[22] Presumably that includes the Kennedy women.

Jackson has spoken out forcefully against "official governmental pressure to thwart desires for children that are both biblical and valid." He is not apologetic that he himself has four children; he does not believe that he is guilty of demographic irresponsibility. In his 1971 judgment, he has no worry about overpopulation in the sense that population increase is outstripping the earth's capacity to produce food. Jackson has boundless confidence in a technology which has rendered "utterly obsolete" such Malthusian theses.[23] Redistribution of the nation's wealth is the great need, he says, not population control. Hunger is the danger, not too many people.

Jackson's passion for greater social justice and economic democracy is laudable. Distributing the vast wealth of the United States on a more equitable basis is long overdue. So is the creation of a truly multiracial society free of racial discrimination. But the need for the United States to adopt and implement a national population policy should not be pooh-poohed particularly by the spokesmen for the poor. America cannot continue to preach population control sermons to the developing nations if we do not simultaneously strive for a stationary population here at home. Famine has ravaged several countries in West Africa and certain

regions of Ethiopia. Asia is threatened with mass starvation and
the United States will have to share its shrinking granary reserves.
Unwanted accretions to our population will only worsen the problem. We, in this country, need both hunger control and birth
control programs. They are not, as Jackson implies, mutually
exclusive. Indeed, family planning will ease the tragedy of hunger
and malnutrition in this land of bounty. It already has.

Jackson is also wary of a national birth control policy by
which the poor and the weak—especially blacks and other
minorities—will be removed or controlled by sophisticated
methods. "Contraceptives," he has foretold, "will become a
form of drug warfare against the helpless in this nation." Obstetric
and gynecology wards in municipal hospitals will be utilized to
liquidate those whom we could not dispose of in the Indochinese
rice paddies.[24]

Who knows that the cure for cancer will not come out of the
mind of some black child, Jackson asks rhetorically in his anti-
abortion rhetoric.[25] Is Jackson seriously suggesting that in the hope
of producing a Nobel laureate in medical science or another Martin
Luther King, Jr., blacks have as many children as possible? If so,
no zygote can be destroyed, no egg should go unfertilized. Black
babies should be manufactured with assembly line regularity.
Surely great black men and women are more likely to be produced
by families having fewer children on whom they can concentrate
their limited energies and resources.

Jesse Jackson, though one of the most dynamic and intelligent
black Americans on the current scene, has expressed several
ill-informed and shortsighted opinions on population questions.
He told the Population Commission in June 1971: "We are
clamoring for birth control in this nation when population has in
fact declined since the 1950s. A simple almanac will attest to that
fact."[26] An almanac would do no such thing. On this fundamental
point Reverend Jackson is dead wrong. During the twenty-year
span 1950 to 1970, the population of the United States rose by well
over fifty million. What Jackson probably confused was the
depression of our national birth rate or the slowdown in our

population growth rate with a nonexistent drop in total population. Not only has our total population not declined, but even stabilization or zero population growth cannot be realized for more than half a century because of the age structure of our present population. In other words, because of an upswing in the number of persons of child-bearing age, an average of two children per family would only mean a deceleration in the rate of population increase, not a reduction in population. For the remainder of the twentieth century, births will surpass deaths. Just as most Americans have never been exposed to information about harsh racial realities in the United States, Jesse Jackson, along with tens of millions of other Americans, has been shielded from basic demographic concepts and data.

As we have seen, several black spokesmen were cynical about the ecological "craze" of the late 1960s of which growing apprehension of a population explosion was one facet. Blacks were worried that national attention and, more important, public money desperately needed in the ghettos, could be diverted to environmental causes. At the First National Congress on Optimum Population and Environment in 1970, the discontented black caucus submitted that "the elimination of dangerous species such as rats, roaches and other vermin is of more immediate concern to Black people than the preservation of brook trout, buffalo and bald eagles." Although the caucus did not reject birth control per se, they pointed out that it was no remedy for the health problems of the living. The caucus also wanted an assurance that "*no coercive* family planning or population stabilization measures are allowed to become part of a national or local legislative policy." Coercion is no academic matter, as we shall see.

## NOTES

1. "Planned Parenthood," *The Crisis* 77, No. 3 (March 1970): 78-79.

2. John Morsell, letter to the author, 24 April 1972.

3. Policy statement approved by the National Urban League's Board of Trustees, 19 November 1962.

4. Whitney M. Young, Jr., *To Be Equal* (New York: McGraw-Hill Book Co., 1964), p. 179.

5. Edwin C. Berry, "The Negro, Poverty and Population," Address delivered at the Planned Parenthood—World-Population Conference in Milwaukee, 7 May 1965.

6. "Watts Extended Health and Family Planning Group Inc.," *The Family Planner*, December 1969, pp. 4-5.

7. Martin Luther King, Jr. *Family Planning—A Special and Urgent Concern* (New York: Planned Parenthood-World Population, n.d.), pp. 3-4.

8. Carl Rowan, "U.S. Family Planning Programs," *Scrantonian*, 28 March 1971.

9. HR 3381, 93d Congress, 1st Session.

10. Ibid.

11. Congresswoman Barbara Jordan, letter to the author, 10 January 1974.

12. *New York Times*, 31 December 1971.

13. Langston Hughes, "Population Explosion," *New York Post*, 10 December 1965.

14. *Providence Journal*, 7 June 1970; *Springfield Sunday Republican*, 7 June 1970.

15. Paul R. Ehrlich, *The Population Bomb* (New York: Ballantine Books, 1968).

16. Edgar Chasteen, "The Stork Is Not the Bird of Paradise." Reprinted from *Mademoiselle*, January 1970.

17. *Yale News*, 27 January 1972.

18. U.S. Commission on Population Growth and the American Future, *Statements at Public Hearings of the Commission on Population Growth and the American Future*. Volume VII of Commission Publications (Washington, D.C.: U.S. Government Printing Office, 1972), p. 40.

19. Ibid., pp. 227-228.

20. Paul R. Ehrlich and Anne H. Ehrlich, "Population Control and Genocide," *New Democratic Coalition Newsletter*, July 1970, p. 5.

21. "Conversation: Jesse Jackson and Marcia Gillespie," *Essence*, July 1971.

22. Ehrlich and Ehrlich, "Population Control and Genocide."

23. *Statements at Public Hearings of the Commission on Population Growth and the American Future*, VII, p. 165.

24. Ibid.

25. Al Rutledge, "Is Abortion Black Genocide?" *Essence*, September 1973, p. 36.

26. *Statements at Public Hearings of the Commission on Population Growth and the American Future*, VII, p. 165. Inexplicably, Jackson told the Commission on the same occasion that the American population had increased 32 percent between 1950 and 1969 (p. 166).

# 10 . Coercion and Society's "Parasites"

Recent history is studded with cases of black and brown minority group members who were pressured to undergo sterilization operations or to limit their fecundity by some other means. In the mid-1960s involuntary sterilization was used by overzealous California judges as a condition of probation. For example, in 1965 Miguel Andrada, who had pleaded guilty to a charge of nonsupport, underwent sterilization rather than serve a term in prison. A regretful Andrada subsequently filed a lawsuit. Making probation contingent upon sterilization, he contended, violated procedural due process and constituted cruel and unusual punishment. Eventually the United States Supreme Court declined to review the case.[1]

Another California case involved Nancy Hernandez, a twenty-one-year-old woman of Mexican-American background, who had pleaded guilty to a misdemeanor. She admitted being present in a room where her common-law husband was illegally smoking marijuana. Mrs. Hernandez, the mother of two young children, was a welfare recipient at the time. She was confronted with the unpalatable choice of probation conditional upon sterilization or,

alternatively, a possible six-month jail sentence. Presiding
municipal judge Frank P. Kearney later informed the press that the
sterilization stipulation was justified because Mrs. Hernandez was
"in danger of continuing to live a dissolute life endangering the
health, safety and lives of her minor children."[2] At first she
reluctantly agreed to the operation. "I didn't know what to say. I
was more or less scared, I had to make a choice," explained the
shocked woman. "I had kids to care for. I didn't want to leave my
kids so I agreed."[3] But then Nancy Hernandez had a change of
heart, whereupon she was given a ninety-day jail term. Happily,
Mrs. Hernandez was only required to serve a few hours of her
sentence because Judge Kearney was reversed on appeal.

In an eminently sound friend of the court brief challenging the
lower court ruling, the American Civil Liberties Union requested
that the sterilization condition of Nancy Hernandez' probation be
declared null and void. The ACLU argued that the imposition of
sterilization as a condition of probation, at least for the offense
committed by Mrs. Hernandez, was invalid. Clearly, the order of
the court was not aimed at averting the birth of defective children.
There was no compelling state interest: "the societal interest in
preventing people from being at a place where marijuana is being
used is not justification for sterilizing an individual who happened
to be there, any more than were the crime involved one of speed-
ing." Furthermore, the sterilization proviso shocked the conscience. It violated "the evolving standards of decency of our
society and [was] an affront to the dignity of man." To the ACLU
it contravened Nancy Hernandez' right of due process and was
cruel and unusual punishment.[4]

On appeal the sterilization requirement was deleted from the
sentence, which was reduced to three years on probation. Superior
Court Justice C. Douglas Smith held that Judge Kearney had acted
"outside the law." Judge Smith was personally in sympathy with
those law-abiding taxpayers who asked "why they should be
called upon to pour their hard-earned tax dollars" into supporting
Mrs. Hernandez' welfare condition. At the same time he recognized that the answer was simple: the law required it. Moreover,

he could not see how sterilization could protect the young woman or anyone else against the danger of becoming an addict.[5]

The Association for Voluntary Sterilization issued a press release regarding the Hernandez case in which it asserted its conviction that a woman's right to her own body was an inalienable right. Therefore, the association found Judge Kearney's position on compulsory sterilization to be "an unreasonable assault on human dignity."

Lawbreakers have always been among the prime candidates for punitive sterilization. Procreation was not declared to be a basic civil right and liberty until 1942. The U.S. Supreme Court made that declaration in a case involving the Habitual Criminal Statute of Oklahoma. That law, providing for the sterilization of certain recidivists, was successfully challenged by a petitioner who had previously been convicted of armed robbery and chicken stealing. The high court invalidated the Oklahoma statute because it ran afoul of the equal protection clause of the Constitution by exempting some criminals, embezzlers for example, while applying its penalties to others such as Jack T. Skinner, the chicken thief. Speaking for the court, Justice William O. Douglas stated that the "power to sterilize, if exercised, may have subtle, far reaching and devastating effects," and warned that in "evil or reckless hands it can cause races or types which are inimical to the dominant group to wither and disappear."[6]

Coercion has not always meant sterilization per se. In still another California case, the *People* v. *Dominguez* (1967), involving a woman found guilty of second-degree robbery, the condition of probation imposed on her was that she not become pregnant until she married. Probation was revoked when the woman did become pregnant. However, a higher court hearing the case on appeal decided that Ms. Dominguez' "pregnancy was unrelated to robbery. Becoming pregnant while unmarried is a misfortune, not a crime."[7] Ms. Dominguez had contended that she used birth control medication but that it had been ineffective. Contraceptive failure was not an indication of criminality, the appellate court further ruled. Finally, the requirement that the defendant not have more illegitimate offspring was held to be unreasonable and invalid as a requirement of probation.

Compulsion in these kinds of matters has not been limited to California; far from it. In 1967 when three young women with out of wedlock offspring sought public assistance in Prince George's County, Maryland, they were promptly arrested. Charges of child neglect were preferred against them. During the neglect proceedings, the judge was ready to supply "some incentive" to unmarried indigent mothers to "employ methods of family control." Intimidation was really what the judge had in mind, for he said bluntly: "I would require them to study and understand methods of birth control and to practice them at the risk of losing their children if they do not." This threat did not turn out to be an empty one. A finding of neglect was made. Various illegitimate youngsters (two of the women involved had three out of wedlock children, one woman had four) were found to be living in an unstable moral environment. The court ordered that the children be taken from their mothers and placed in foster homes.

Claiming that the crucial issue in the case was that of free choice versus compulsion in birth control, Planned Parenthood filed a friend of the court brief when the matter was appealed to a higher court. Although it tirelessly labors to spread information about family planning as widely as possible, Planned Parenthood is unalterably opposed to any governmental efforts to force family planning on persons unwilling to accept it. In threatening to punish mothers who failed to practice birth control efficiently, the trial court in Prince George's County was violating constitutional rights, including the right of privacy. That right was first enunciated by the Supreme Court in *Griswold* v. *Connecticut* when it decided that the state of Connecticut could not prohibit the use of contraceptives. Neither could a Maryland court require their use without infringing on the same right of privacy, Planned Parenthood argued.[8] Ironically, voluntary planned parenthood services for poor women had been rather meager in the region.

It was the opinion of the appeal court that the state's action in depriving the parents of their out of wedlock children had not been taken to serve the best interests of the youngsters "but rather impermissibly to use the children as pawns in a plan to punish their mothers for their past promiscuity and discourage them and other females of like weaknesses and inclinations from future productivity."[9] The lower court order was reversed and the children were returned to their parents.

Recipients of public assistance are periodically the targets of public officials who see coercive sterilization as an efficient tool in solving social problems. Across the country these men, reflecting the wave of popular indignation over escalating welfare costs, have put forward punitive proposals. These measures have often been seriously debated in state legislatures. Typically, they provide for mandatory sterilization after a woman on welfare has given birth to a certain number of illegitimate children. Continued eligibility for welfare payments depends on compliance. Failure to comply can mean imprisonment according to some of these measures.

Punitive sterilization bills have been introduced in the Mississippi state legislature since 1958, ostensibly to solve the problem of black illegitimacy. State Representative David H. Glass, sponsor of a 1958 bill, did not conceal his purposes. He was angered by black women who made it a business to give birth to illegitimate children and collected welfare assistance for them. Glass wanted "to stop, or slow down, such traffic at its source."[10] Four times more black children than whites were receiving Aid to Families with Dependent Children (AFDC) in Mississippi in the early 1960s. In 1962 the segregationist state welfare commissioner asked pointedly, "how much longer will the white population of Mississippi consent to be taxed and drained of its substance for the benefit of a race, and a nation, which shows no appreciation for their sacrifice."[11] Two years hence a measure passed by the Mississippi house stipulated that any person who became the parent of a second out of wedlock child would be guilty of a felony punishable by a sentence of one to three years in the state penitentiary. A subsequent conviction would be punishable by three to five years in prison. However, a convicted parent had the option of submitting to sterilization in lieu of imprisonment.

The bill was sharply denounced by Dr. Alan F. Guttmacher, president of Planned Parenthood, by the Association for Voluntary Sterilization, and by the Student Nonviolent Coordinating Committee. Quick to recognize the racist overtones of the bill, SNCC issued a pamphlet aptly entitled *Genocide in Mississippi*. SNCC pointed out that one advocate of the measure had offered statistics purporting to show that illegitimacy was more common among black people than among whites. "Parasitical" welfare recipients were chastised during the floor debate, and some backers of the bill made it clear that they hoped passage would lead to an exodus of indigent blacks. "When the cutting starts, they'll [Negroes] head for Chicago," prophesied Representative Stone Barefield, an attorney from Hattiesburg. SNCC interpreted the bill as an effort to lower the black population of Mississippi by destroying their reproductive potential and by forcing them to migrate. It was nothing less than an "experiment in genocide." [12] The SNCC pamphlet described one of the sponsors of the mandatory sterilization proposal as a staff assistant to Senator James O. Eastland, a long-time Negrophobe. It also argued that enactment of the bill by the Mississippi house was facilitated by United States congressional dereliction of duty which left black residents of Mississippi effectively disfranchised. The remedy was federal civil rights legislation that would safeguard the black franchise.

Many southern whites were inclined to see the blacks as an unwelcome element in their midst. Long politically impotent and consequently politically restless, blacks were increasingly eyed with anxiety by the white power structure. In addition, many of the jobs traditionally performed by rural unskilled and unschooled blacks had been automated out of existence by the 1960s. Modern technology had thus rendered the blacks economically useless. Mississippi whites and their elected representatives looked on their departure from the magnolia state as a much hoped-for dividend.

Less and less blacks are viewed as a source of cheap labor. More and more they are seen as a public welfare expense. Ballooning welfare appropriations are the real genesis of punitive sterilization bills. Representative Lucius N. Porth, a Republican in the South Carolina legislature, wrote a 1971 bill directed at female public assistance recipients who had already borne two children. Under its stern provisions the welfare mother would be sterilized or would forfeit her welfare payments. Citizens were irate about the huge sums being squandered on poor relief, Porth said. Welfare families with as many as nine children were a threat to society. They were an expense which the public ought not to have to bear. It was high time that action was taken against people who had children because of "their lust for sex." Porth's proposal won him accolades from ultra-conservative quarters. *The Thunderbolt*, a voice of the National States Rights party, categorically rejects the idea that welfare is a right. Taxpayers "should not have to subsidize the breeding of illegitimate Blacks by lazy people who do not want to work." Industrious whites should not have to finance the "breeding of low caste beings who grow up to become enemies of society." Not unexpectedly, Porth's legislation drew the fire of civil libertarians and civil rights groups. A spokesman for the American Friends Service Committee called it "ridiculous and authoritarian." The leader of the NAACP in South Carolina said the bill was "an attempt to employ Hitler type tactics upon the poor."[13]

In 1973 Larry Bates, a member of the Tennessee House of Representatives, introduced a measure to restrict welfare payments in the volunteer state. Any female who became the mother of more than two illegitimate children would no longer be entitled to receive monthly relief benefits for her additional children beyond two, unless she first agreed to and submitted herself to a sterilization operation. If, after the second illegitimate child, the mother refused to have the operation, then each illegitimate child beyond two would be declared a dependent, destitute, or orphan child. After participating in statewide hearings on welfare problems, Representative Bates felt that his legislation would alleviate a situation that was both detrimental to the well-being of the children involved and an unnecessary drain of taxpayers' dollars.[14]

However, the Department of Public Welfare held that the policies contemplated by Bates would be inconsistent with federal social security laws. If the measures were passed, Tennessee could conceivably lose the federal government's share of Aid to Families with Dependent Children (AFDC) moneys, more than $56 million in 1973-1974 alone. This may explain why the Tennessee House of Representatives never took any action on the bill. Rather than compassion for the indigent or constitutional scruples, the fear of having to bear the welfare burden without the largesse of Washington, D.C., may explain the failure of a single state to enact coercive sterilization of welfare mothers into law.

Punitive sterilization measures are by no means confined to the South. Webber Borcher, a Republican in the Illinois General Assembly, has also authored legislation to limit, by coercion, the fertility of welfare recipients. Upon the birth of a second child, a welfare mother, married or single, would have been required to undergo a tubal ligation. Failure to cooperate would have meant a loss of eligibility for public assistance. Borcher does not "care how many times you go to bed or who you go to bed with [but] you don't have the right to make me pay for it." His contention is that persons on relief are, in truth, wards of the state. Citizens who are being asked to foot the bill therefore have a right to restrict the procreative activities of others.[15] This argument overlooks the possibility that the welfare mother who is permanently neutered today may be self-supporting in the future.

Borcher's measure was blocked by black legislators and their white liberal colleagues. Harold Washington, a black representative from Chicago, found Borcher's bid to write forced sterilization into law frighteningly reminiscent of Nazism.[16]

In the 1973-1974 legislative session Borcher introduced a voluntary sterilization bill. It called for a free vasectomy or tubal ligation for any person eighteen years of age or over who filed with the Department of Public Aid an affidavit attesting to a desire for the operation and an inability to pay for it. This free choice bill would appear to be unobjectionable, but Borcher admits that it is an "attempt to put a foot in the door." One day, he hopes, it can be used as a building block for better control of the welfare problem. "You might say the planting of a tree which I am sure will grow in the future," wrote Borcher, scrambling his figures of speech.[17] Given the representative's record of interest in coercion, it is a tree which will deserve close watching.

Regardless of their opinions about family planning and population control, black spokesmen are adamantly opposed to the forced sterilization of welfare mothers. Despite his pro birth control stand, Julius Lester considers it to be a genocidal weapon against the Afro-American community.[18] Jesse Jackson rightly considers it to be "an inhuman social proposition based upon race rather than population."[19]

Ohio was the locus of another bid to write forced sterilization into law. State representative Gene Damschroder had made a pledge to his constituents that he would take a revolutionary approach to the welfare dilemma. To that end Damschroder deposited two bills in the legislative hopper in 1973. One required the sterilization of welfare mothers if they received public assistance for more than two out of wedlock children. A companion measure provided for the sterilization of fathers who failed to support their minor children. Damschroder conceded that his proposals were draconian but necessary to cope with the "welfare mess" and escalating tax burdens. Damschroder dramatized the fact that aid to families with dependent children, the type of public assistance which benefits welfare mothers and their offspring, exceeded the appropriation for primary and secondary schooling in Ohio.

Damschroder finds it difficult to think of public charges as fully human. "If a man decides to live like an animal," the legislator has said, "he should be treated like an animal."[20]

Damschroder met stiff resistance both inside and outside the Democratically controlled legislature. A spokesman for the American Civil Liberties Union called his sterilization suggestions

"Neanderthal," "outrageous," and "unconstitutional."[21] Governor John J. Gilligan's press secretary commented, "People who introduce bills like that neither understand the welfare problem nor want to."[22] Neither bill was ever assigned to a committee for consideration.

It is abundantly clear that Damschroder is not alone in his thinking, not in Ohio, not in the country as a whole. Eighty-nine percent of the sample in a straw poll conducted by the Elyna, Ohio, *Chronicle Telegram* in April 1973 favored the sterilization remedy. While such one-sided results raise serious doubts about the reliability and validity of the poll, unquestionably a sizable segment of public opinion leans to the hard-line Damschroder approach. Nor are his supporters to be dismissed out of hand as dyed in the wool bigots of the Archie Bunker school of thought.

Deeply frustrated by runaway inflation which inexorably shrinks their hard-earned dollars, many Americans seize upon welfare costs as a scapegoat. Significantly, astronomical defense expenditures are ignored altogether. "Giveaways" to the needy evoke more coarse epithets than loopholes in our income tax system which allow many of the rich to pay nominal taxes or no taxes at all. "Welfare chiselers," not Pentagon generals or tax-evading millionaires, are the objects of the public's pent-up hostility. In this context, punitive sterilization as a solution to the complex and seemingly insoluble welfare conundrum has struck responsive chords in those who see themselves as decent hard-working citizens who pay their debts and taxes and are weary of supporting those whom they see as lazy ne'er-do-wells who spend their time and energy fornicating and "boozing." That welfare recipients are living comfortable, even luxurious lives complete with color television and brightly hued Cadillacs becomes an article of faith. Popular bromides about welfare, inextricably bound up as they are with sexual and racial mythology, die slowly.

This is not to say that welfare is not a problem of upsetting magnitude. In the 1960s, the decade of the civil rights movement and the black revolution, the number of relief recipients in the AFDC category grew by a whopping 225 percent. In 1961 the total number of AFDC recipients was 3,566,000. Ten years later that figure had grown to 10,653,000.[23] Upwards of eleven million Americans were receiving help in this category in 1972. Needy mothers, those who are widowed, divorced, separated, or unwed, and their dependent children are the beneficiaries of this governmental aid. As interpreted by many Americans, ''handouts'' to such people are subsidies to immorality, bonuses to whores and their bastards who are feeding, generation after generation, at the public trough.

Popular opinion which holds that the welfare problem and the Negro problem are synonymous is based on misinformation. Demographic data supplied by the Department of Health, Education and Welfare show that in 1971 43.3 percent of the families getting AFDC were black as compared with 48.3 percent of the recipient families who were white. It is true that black AFDC families tend to be larger than white AFDC families. It is also true that there is a grossly disproportionate representation of blacks on the welfare rolls, a reflection of centuries of enslavement and degradation. But the belief that the welfare problem would vanish if Afro-Americans vanished is a pipe dream as the foregoing statistics indicate.

Race is never mentioned in punitive sterilization bills. That would be a clearcut contravention of the fourteenth amendment to the United States Constitution. But blacks are represented on the welfare rolls out of all proportion to their percentage of the overall population. To that extent an involuntary sterilization requirement would disproportionately affect Afro-Americans. Because of stereotypical misconceptions of black laziness and black sexual appetites, legislators may find it somewhat easier to support such drastic actions where the black welfare population is substantial. On the other hand it is entirely possible, given the lawmakers' desire to eliminate needless ''charity'' that the same bills would be introduced even if Afro-Americans were not conspicuous among relief recipients. In 1973 a welfare sterilization measure was advanced in the New Hampshire state legislature; blacks are an infinitesimal fraction of the population in the granite state.

Welfare "parasitism" is also of concern to solons in the nation's capital. As chairman of the Senate Finance Committee Senator Russell Long has excoriated welfare mothers who sit around their houses all day long drinking liquor, too lazy "to pick up a beer can" or "even catch a rat." He has blasted those who do not feel like doing anything, "not even slapping at a fly." The Louisiana Democrat made his acidulous comments in 1967 in regard to a proposal to make job training mandatory for women receiving AFDC. "I don't feel like paying people for doing nothing," he exclaimed.[24] Long was speaking for the millions of Americans whose understanding of the welfare quagmire in which welfare mothers are immersed is simplistic at best.

In the early 1970s Spiro T. Agnew, then still a heartbeat away from the presidency, also addressed himself to the need to make "hard social judgments" about the welfare problem. After his election Agnew's verbal assaults on effete snobs, academicians, and the liberal press had made his theretofore unfamiliar name a household word. Those were triumphant days for the vice-president. His own disgrace and precipitous fall from power were not visible on the political horizon. Agnew eagerly served as the sanctimonious mouthpiece for middle-class, middle American morality. Wrongdoers and the indolent indigent had to be dealt with sternly. Agnew's gross insensitivity to the poor was plainly exhibited on that celebrated occasion when he remarked that if you have seen one ghetto you have seen them all. In January 1971 with righteous indignation, he asked rhetorically who was going to tell a welfare mother with three or four out of wedlock children, all charges of the state, "We're very sorry but we will not be able to allow you to have more children."[25] Agnew's comments fell short of advocating coercive sterilization.

If the welfare crisis deepens and if the taxpayers' burden grows still heavier, publicly elected officials will surely turn to mandatory sterilization in greater numbers. Its appeal is simple and Americans love simple, easy, quick solutions to complex problems. It holds out the possibility of cutting the Gordian knot of welfare with the surgeon's scalpel. It is a solution which means substantially fewer welfare checks and fewer welfare checks will mean lower taxes—hopefully. But mandatory sterilization of careless or imprudent welfare mothers is of dubious constitutionality and an insult to human dignity. Moreover, seen in the light of society's muleheaded resistance to making *voluntary* birth control, including sterilization, readily available to the general public, it is blatantly hypocritical.

*Muhammad Speaks* deliberately obfuscated the difference between punitive sterilization and truly voluntary birth control in a story about the white supremacist National States Rights Party (NSRP). Involuntary sterilization has been enthusiastically endorsed by the NSRP which also favors stripping blacks of their United States citizenship and deporting them to Africa. Fearful that white American society will be destroyed if black Americans continue "breeding like rats," the NSRP has called for legislation to curtail the black birth rate. Black families would be limited to one or two offspring. Black parents exceeding this quota would be sterilized, as would their surplus children. Black parents of illegitimate children would be made sterile under the proposed legislation, as would blacks who had children while on public assistance. Black criminals and black mental defectives would suffer the same fate. *Muhammad Speaks* is correct in describing these insidious ideas as "neo-Nazi." But in asserting that such right-wing racist rantings show the true nature of birth control, the Muslim organ is distorting the truth. There is no resemblance between the motivation of the NSRP and that of Planned Parenthood. There is no similarity between the language of the NSRP and that of federal and state government officials concerning birth control. There is hardly a scintilla of evidence that racists of that ilk are largely influencing current government family planning programs, as *Muhammad Speaks* claimed.[26] Still, when bigots endorse forcible sterilization, voluntary sterilization becomes a highly suspect proposal. The whole question of coercive sterilization, sex-related and race-related as it is, is a highly emotional one likely to elicit visceral, not cerebral, responses.

Even voluntary sterilization proposals are suspect when they are put forward by persons who are tainted with racism. Such a person is Professor William Shockley, who was awarded a Nobel Prize in 1956 for his invention of the transistor. Though he lacks the credentials of a qualified geneticist, Shockley has not been diffident about expounding his genetic theories. Shockley's research has led him inescapably to the conclusion that the ''major cause of American Negroes' intellectual and social deficits is heredity and is racially genetic in origin.'' That being the case their deficits cannot be remedied to any significant degree by improving the environment. Shockley has argued that the genetically disadvantaged, principally but not exclusively the blacks, are reproducing disproportionately. Welfare programs which encourage the least fit, the least effective, and the least intelligent segments of our population to have large families have fostered this dysgenic trend. Dysgenics meaning retrogressive evolution is the opposite of eugenics. To cope with this sad situation Shockley has proposed as a ''thinking exercise'' a voluntary sterilization bonus plan. Those individuals with substandard IQ's and other genetic disabilities would be paid cash bonuses for being sterilized. Shockley contends that, if $1,000 were paid for each point below 100 IQ, ''$30,000 put in trust for a 70 I.Q. moron potentially capable of producing twenty children might return $250,000 to taxpayers in reduced costs of mental retardation care.''[27]

The sterilization plan for which Shockley would like a trial run would not apply just to blacks. Bonuses would be available regardless of race, sex, or welfare status. But black critic Dr. Frances Welsing of Howard University reminds us that blacks in a white-dominated society are peculiarly vulnerable and unable to protect themselves against abuses.[28] While Professor Shockley reassures doubters that there would be no atrocities, Roy Innis of CORE has labeled the voluntary sterilization bonus plan ''genocidal.''[29]

Sterilization atrocities amounting to genocide would not be unprecedented. The Nazis waged a sterilization war against the biologically inferior. Even before the onset of World War II, perhaps two hundred thousand mentally retarded people and additional thousands of schizophrenics, epileptics, and alcoholics were compulsorily sterilized.[30] Sterilization was a basic component of Hitler's final solution of the Jewish problem. To perfect operating techniques, Jews in death camps were subjected to various kinds of experimental sexual surgery, much of it done without any anesthetics. In one experiment the genitalia were irradiated, and then the ovaries and testicles were surgically excised to assess the results.

So the precedent is there and blacks know it. Yesterday it happened to the Jews and to the mentally and physically defective in Nazi Germany. Maybe tomorrow it will happen to black Americans in the United States. Some blacks believe that it has already happened in unrecorded isolated cases.

Rumors are often circulated about black women who have been sterilized without any medical necessity for the procedure. They are widely believed by blacks. "Mississippi appendectomy" is a euphemism for a tubal ligation or hysterectomy performed on southern black women without their consent and for no good health reason. Of course, existence of the expression indicates not that the practice is commonplace but that it is thought to be so. Precise data on such operations are virtually impossible to come by. Fannie Lou Hamer has provided one estimate.

For many years Fannie Lou Hamer toiled as a sharecropper on Mississippi plantations. A woman whose native intelligence and sheer grit enabled her to become a leader of the biracial Mississippi Freedom Democratic party, Mrs. Hamer shocked an audience in 1965 when she stated that 60 percent of the black women taken to Sunflower (Mississippi) City Hospital were sterilized there without any valid medical reason. Frequently they were not informed that they had been made infertile until they were discharged from the hospital.[31] Regrettably, Mrs. Hamer provided no evidence on that occasion or subsequently.

Most allegations of this nature are never substantiated. Nevertheless, an indeterminate number of sterilizations have been performed either for financial or racist reasons, or for both. Dr.

Herbert Avery of the Watts Extended Health and Family Planning Group claims to have examined numerous black southern women who had been sterilized without their consent "because they were having too many children."[32]

Naomi T. Gray told a Mini-Consultation on the Mental and Physical Health Problems of Black Women held in Washington, D.C., in 1974 that over a long period of time she had encountered a "substantial" number of black women who had been "sterilized through means of deceit and trickery." When most of these women put their signatures on consent forms, they were not knowingly agreeing to be sterilized. They were simply "placing their faith in the doctor to discover and rectify the so-called trouble."[33]

Black physician Edgar B. Keemer, Jr., who operates a clinic in Detroit, has pioneered in nonhospital, therapeutic pregnancy termination for thirty years. He has seen "several" patients who had been to other clinics and had been talked into sterilization at the same time they had abortions or as a necessary prerequisite for abortion. Unfortunately, Dr. Keemer, a champion of freedom of choice, has not been able to convince these women to come forward to talk about their experiences. They were anxious to forget about what had happened and wanted to avoid publicity. Dr. Keemer firmly believes that the practice of encouraging the patient to have a sterilization operation along with the abortion is "far more prevalent than we realize." He is convinced that greed—the gynecologist thereby obtains two fees—and subconscious racism are the underlying motives.[34]

Apart from avarice and subconscious or conscious racism, there may be another factor that prompts physicians to persuade patients to be sterilized. Subjects for surgical teaching programs are usually in short supply. Consequently, residents in city hospitals allegedly turn to the dependent poor to meet the demand. Case data compiled by medical students at Boston City Hospital, a teaching hospital for three medical schools, indicate that patients have been coaxed into consenting to a hysterectomy in lieu of a tubal ligation. Residents like to do hysterectomies, one confessed, "It's more of a challenge . . . a well-trained chimpanzee can do tubal ligations . . . and it's good experience for the junior resident.'' This grave charge was leveled in a study prepared by the Health Research Group in Washington, D.C., a public interest, nonprofit enterprise funded by Ralph Nader's Public Citizen, Inc.[35]

It was not the first time such accusations had been made against Boston City Hospital. A report by medical students finding fault with the substandard patient care in the obstetrical and gynecological department was the subject of a front page story in the *Boston Globe* in April 1972. Two specific complaints were (1) that excessive and medically unnecessary surgery was performed to give residents and interns the surgical training which they desired, and (2) that surgery consent forms were signed under duress and without adequate explanation given to the patient. There were clearcut racial overtones to the indictment: the medical students were upset over the possibility that Afro-Americans and Spanish-speaking women might be sterilized more frequently by hysterectomy while white women were more likely to be sterilized by tubal ligation, a less drastic procedure.[36] When queried about the *Boston Globe* story, Francis E. Guiney, the executive director of Boston's Department of Health and Hospitals, replied that the records of the Patient Care Committee which had explored this serious matter were confidential and could not be released. However, he did state that the concerns expressed by the medical students were ''thoroughly reviewed and could not be substantiated.''[37]

At the Baltimore City Hospital, a dozen women were asked to consent to sterilization only minutes before a Caeserian section and the sterilization procedure were to be performed. The source of this information was Dr. Bernard Rosenfeld of the Health Research Group, who had first-hand knowledge of these incidents. These were allegedly cases in which the patients had not previously indicated a desire to be rendered incapable of bearing additional children. Clinic authorities normally inquired about possible patient interest in sterilization weeks or months before delivery, but not in these cases.[38] If the allegations are true, twelve patients committed themselves to sterilization when they were not free agents. In such circumstances the attendant benefits and risks could not possibly be weighed with appropriate care. The patients may not have known that the sterilizations were permanent in effect. Because he never received a direct or indirect communication from the Nader group, the director of obstetrics and gynecology at the Baltimore City Hospital declined to refute these allegations in detail. In a letter to this author he chose instead "to ignore incomplete and partially inaccurate information."[39]

Dr. Rosenfeld has also charged that hysterectomies were carried out unnecessarily at Los Angeles County Hospital and that tubal ligations were encouraged not for the sake of the patients, but rather to give future physicians additional practice in surgery. Dr. Rosenfeld has further reported that of more than twenty-five residents and interns surveyed at Los Angeles County Hospital, more than 50 percent stated that, in the hospitals where they had trained before going to Los Angeles, "there was considerable 'pushing' of elective sterilization and 'hard-selling' of these procedures to women."[40]

A hospital official in Los Angeles gave the most candid reply to the allegations of Dr. Rosenfeld and the Health Research Group, saying that "there are kernels of truth and areas of gross over-interpretation." He admitted that occasionally the subject of sterilization had been discussed with the patients for the first time when entering labor, a wholly inappropriate moment for making properly informed decisions. That procedure has now been stopped, he said. Language difficulties were blamed for mis-understandings between physicians and patients regarding the consequences of tubal interruption. Seventy-five percent of all patients at the hospital are Chicanos, only 10 percent black Americans. The hospital official also admitted that an extremely small number of patients regretted their sterilization after having elected to have the operation under stress or based on a mis-apprehension.[41]

Under the joint auspices of the American Public Health Associa-

tion and the American College of Obstetricians and Gyne-
cologists, a study was done in 1967 examining the contraceptive,
abortion, and sterilization services of teaching hospitals. One
astounding finding of the study was that 53.6 percent of teaching
hospitals nationwide made sterilization a requirement for winning
approval for an abortion. Still more astounding is the failure of any
of these coercive "package deals" to lead to litigation charging
infringement of constitutional rights.[42]

Furtive, forcible sterilization is an old story in the United States.
Several years before the Tuskegee venereal disease project began,
Public Health Service physicians and others operated syphilis
treatment clinics in Macon County, Alabama, and elsewhere in the
rural South. Any and all black women discovered to have syphilis
were sterilized, it has been alleged. One investigator has guessed
that as many as a thousand such women were neutered in Macon
County alone. Many of these women were perfectly capable of
giving birth to normal, healthy babies after being cured, but this
was ignored. A physician associated with the project in its initial
stages glibly rationalized the routine sterilization practice: "we
hope also to cut down on the tremendous loss of life by mis-
carriages and in early childhood."[43]

It is abundantly clear that, for many years, some women, black
and brown-skinned women in particular, have had their tubes tied
or their wombs removed without any medical necessity for the
surgery. Exactly how many is not known. In all probability we will
always be in the dark about the scope of this medical and racial
atrocity. But even one such case is an outrage which no civilized
society can tolerate.

## NOTES

1. This and a number of other related cases are discussed in Elyce
Zenoff Ferster, "Eliminating the Unfit—Is Sterilization the Answer?"
*Ohio State Law Journal* 27 (1966): 591-633.

2. *Augusta Chronicle*, 25 May 1966; *Washington Post*, 25 May
1966.

3. *Los Angeles Times*, 31 May 1966.

4. Brief in re: Nancy Hernandez, #76757 Superior Court for the County of Santa Barbara, State of California, 27 May 1966.

5. *San Francisco Chronicle*, 9 June 1966.

6. *Skinner* v. *Oklahoma*, 316 U.S. 535 (1942).

7. *People* v. *Dominguez*, 64 California Rptr. 290 (1967).

8. Brief in re: Barbara Jean Cager et al., Court of Appeals of Maryland, 353 September Term, 1967.

9. In re: Cager et al., 251 Maryland 473 (1967), p. 480.

10. See Julius Paul, "The Return of Punitive Sterilization Proposals—Current Attacks on Illegitimacy and the AFDC Program," *Law and Society Review* 3, No. 1 (August 1968): 89. Glass' statements were in a letter to Julius Paul.

11. Quoted in Edgar May, *The Wasted Americans—Cost of Our Welfare Dilemma* (New York: Harper and Row, Publishers, 1964), p. 14.

12. *Genocide in Mississippi* (Atlanta: The Student Nonviolent Coordinating Committee, n.d.), pp. 4-5. Included in the pamphlet was a copy of Article II of the UN's genocide convention listing the various acts which constituted genocide. The reader's attention was drawn to the convention's reference to "imposing measures intended to prevent births within the group."

13. *New York Times*, 23 April 1971; *The Thunderbolt*, June 1971.

14. Larry Bates, letter to the author, 28 March 1974.

15. Webber Borcher, letter to the author, 23 May 1974.

16. *New York Times*, 23 May 1971.

17. Webber Borcher, letter to the author, 23 May 1974.

18. Julius Lester, "Birth Control and Blacks," in *Revolutionary Notes* (New York: Richard W. Baron, 1969), p. 140.

19. "Conversation: Jesse Jackson and Marcia Gillespie," *Essence*, July 1971.

20. *Cincinnati Post and Times Star*, 25 April 1973.

21. Ibid. and *The* [Toledo] *Blade*, 19 April 1973.

22. *The* [Cleveland] *Plain Dealer*, 20 April 1973.

23. *Social Security Bulletin—Annual Statistical Bulletin 1971* (Washington, D.C.: Department of Health, Education and Welfare, 1971).

24. *The Washington Star*, 22 September 1967.

25. *New York Times*, 15 January 1971.

26. *Muhammad Speaks*, 26 December 1969. The attitudes of the NSRP were taken from their pamphlet, *Negro Birth Rate Dangers*.

27. William Shockley, "Dysgenics, Geneticity, Raceology: A Challenge to the Intellectual Responsibility of Education," A Special Supplement of the *Phi Delta Kappan*, January 1972, p. 306.

28. Dr. Welsing made her remarks on the "Black Journal" program on WGBH-TV on 19 February 1974.

29. John J. O'Connor, "TV: Shockley versus Innis," *New York Times*, 13 December 1973.

30. Richard Grünberger, *The 12-Year Reich—A Social History of Nazi Germany* (New York: Holt, Rinehart and Winston Inc., 1971), p. 225.

31. *Washington Post*, 27 January 1965.

32. *Los Angeles Times*, 30 September 1968.

33. "Stresses and Strains on Black Women," *Ebony*, June 1974, p. 36.

34. Dr. Edgar B. Keemer, Jr., letter to the author, 5 January 1974.

35. Bernard Rosenfeld, Sidney M. Wolfe, and Robert E. McGarrah, Jr., "A Health Research Group Study on Surgical Sterilization: Present Abuses and Proposed Regulations," Unpublished report, 29 October 1973, p. 3.

36. *Boston Globe*, 29 April 1972.

37. Francis E. Guiney, letter to the author, 11 January 1974.

38. Rosenfeld et al., "A Health Research Group Study on Surgical Sterilization," p. 4.

39. Dr. Frank Kaltreider, letter to the author, 5 March 1974.

40. Rosenfeld, et al., "A Health Research Group Study on Surgical Sterilization," pp. 7-8.

41. E. J. Quilligan, letter to the author, 29 March 1974.

42. Johan W. Eliot, Robert E. Hall, J. Robert Willson, and Carolyn Houser, "The Obstetrician's View," in ed. Robert E. Hall *Abortion in a Changing World*, (New York: Columbia University Press, 1970), I, 93.

43. Henry Leifermann, "They Still Think Sterilization Is Good Enough for Welfare Mothers," *Southern Voices* 1, No. 2 (May-June 1974): 79; and Henry Leifermann, letter to the author, 29 July 1974.

# 11 . *Sterilization, Genocide, and the Black American*

Over the years sterilization has been one of those very delicate subjects which television has carefully avoided, fearful that a segment of the mass audience would be offended no matter how gingerly the subject was handled. It is mainly because of its religious overtones that sterilization has been virtually taboo to networks all too ready to cave in to popular protest. Yet, in a single month, February 1974, a couple of programs radically changed the time-honored network attitude of "the less said the better." First, on February 3 the Columbia Broadcasting System's public affairs program "Sixty Minutes" included a story on coercive sterilization. Less than two weeks later the American Broadcasting Company's weekly series, "Owen Marshall, Attorney-at-Law," treated this highly sensitive topic in an hour-long dramatic presentation. The Owen Marshall episode dealt with a flint-hearted, overzealous physician determined to sterilize a resistant teenage patient, Judy Simpson. The girl was a borderline retarded black youngster whose befuddled mother had been talked into giving her legal sanction to the operation. Previously, the viewers are told, the same doctor, concerned about overpopulation in the world, had coaxed another young girl into submitting to a tubal ligation. Disconsolate, that girl had attempted suicide. Owen Marshall is successful in preventing a similar tragedy in Judy Simpson's case.

National television's abrupt about-face on the sterilization question resulted directly from the extensive press coverage given to a handful of celebrated cases of forcible sterilization. Those cases brought a concealed practice to public view and simultaneously caused a thundercloud of controversy.

Reference has previously been made to the anonymity treasured by the vast majority of poor women who believe that they were tricked into undergoing sterilization operations which they neither needed nor wanted. There are notable exceptions. One black victim of an involuntary sterilization who has come forward, determined to right a social wrong not only for herself but for others in similarly vulnerable positions, is Nial Ruth Cox. With the help of American Civil Liberties Union attorneys, Miss Cox, now a nurse's aide in a Long Island hospital, has filed suit to have a North Carolina sterilization statute declared unconstitutional. She has also asked for one million dollars in damages to compensate her for the physical and emotional injuries she has suffered as a result of the sterilization procedure performed on her.[1]

At the time of her operation in February 1965 Miss Cox was living with her eight siblings and her mother, a welfare recipient, in North Carolina. Her father was deceased. Though unmarried, Miss Cox had given birth to a child in 1964, when she was seventeen years of age. Miss Cox contends that when her daughter was conceived she had no access to birth control information and devices. Pregnancy interruption, even if it had not been contrary to her moral and philosophical beliefs, was hardly an option, as North Carolina law prohibited abortion.

When Miss Cox turned eighteen she was no longer entitled to receive welfare benefits. Nevertheless, she alleges that a caseworker stated that because of her "immorality," she would have to be sterilized *temporarily* or her mother, her brothers, and sisters would all be stricken from the welfare rolls. Such an eventuality was unthinkable as their living conditions, even with welfare, were primitive. They had no electric lights, no stove, no refrigerator in their home. Under North Carolina law, if the parent of a mental defective under twenty-one years of age gives her approval, consent to be sterilized need not be obtained from the minor herself. Consent never was obtained in Miss Cox's case. Nor was she told that the operation was irreversible and that she would be rendered permanently, not temporarily, infertile. After the operation a physician informed her that she had no cause to worry. She was reassured that in the future she would be able to have more children. In effect, Miss Cox claims that she was told barefaced lies. Furthermore, in 1973, Miss Cox told an interviewer that her mother did not comprehend the real implications of giving her approval for the operation. "Nobody explained anything. They treated us as though we were animals."[2]

No steps were ever taken to verify that Nial Ruth Cox was "feebleminded" and she steadfastly insists that she is not "now and never has been mentally defective or incompetent." Her suit further asserts that no evidence was ever advanced to show that a sterilization operation "would be for the best interest of the mental, moral or physical improvement of plaintiff and/or for the public good." Why then was she subjected to an "irreversible bilateral partial salpingectomy sterilization" instead of being fitted with an intrauterine device as her mother had been? Her brief says that because of her mother's status as an adult certain rights could not be cavalierly brushed aside. For instance, hearings procedures would be required. But the plaintiff was not just black, female, an unwed mother, and a welfare family member. She was also a minor and as such was not entitled to safeguards under North Carolina law.

Because of her operation Miss Cox asserts that she has suffered serious physical disabilities and severe mental depression. When she told her fiancé that she could never again bear children, he terminated their engagement. He did not want half a woman, an embittered Miss Cox explained. Her induced barrenness, she feels, sharply reduces her chances of attaining marriage and a normal family life for which she yearns. Most men are reluctant to marry sterile women.

Asked why she had been willing to publicize her ordeal, Miss Cox replied: "They want to stop Black people from having children . . . It's a disgrace. I hope and pray they won't go any further with this thing."[3]

"This thing" has not just had an impact on blacks. Evidently other poverty-stricken nonwhIte women, and sometimes poor whites, have also fallen prey to the sterilizing scalpel. A little publicized case involving the alleged forcible sterilization of an American Indian woman is now being litigated in Pennsylvania. Welfare officials and physicians in the Pittsburgh area are the defendants in a lawsuit brought by Norma Jean Serena whose sole means of support is furnished by the Department of Public Welfare. Mrs. Serena is a divorced mother of five children, two legitimate, three illegitimate. One of her children is currently institutionalized because of mental retardation.

In 1970 a bilateral salpingectomy was performed on Mrs. Serena, leaving her unable ever to conceive and bear a child again. Her lawyer contends that the operation was done without the plaintiff's knowledge or consent, that it was not necessary for her health or safety, and that she did not even learn about the operation until several days later. Norma Jean was then told that she had produced enough children and that any subsequent pregnancies might have eventuated in the birth of a deformed or retarded offspring.

Three of Mrs. Serena's children were also taken from her and placed in foster homes. She has since had to engage in a protracted struggle to regain the custody of her children.

In his amended complaint, Richard Steven Levine, counsel to Mrs. Serena, claims that several of his client's constitutional rights have been flouted: to maintain a family relationship; to have the custody, companionship, services, and affection of her minor children; to procreate and bear children; and other rights as well. Compensatory and punitive damages are being sought.[4]

Reports of sterilization through intimidation coming out of

South Carolina helped to precipitate a great hue and cry in 1973. Pregnant low-income residents of Aiken County, each already the mother of three children, were virtually compelled to go elsewhere for obstetrical care unless they were willing to be sterilized. This became public knowledge when Mrs. Carol Brown, a white mother of four, disclosed that in order to have her fifth child delivered in Aiken County she would have to consent to a sterilization operation. Those were the terms set by obstetrician Clovis H. Pierce whose motive was to shorten the public assistance rolls. The two other Aiken obstetricians adopted essentially the same policy. Mrs. Brown's husband was serving a prison term for grand larceny. Because of Mr. Brown's incarceration his wife was forced to live on welfare, and expenses incurred by the birth of their expected fifth child would have been met by Medicaid. Mrs. Brown, who balked at Dr. Pierce's stiff terms, was treated by a physician in nearby Augusta, Georgia.[5]

Similar accusations of coercion were made shortly thereafter by other pregnant welfare mothers. Marietta Williams, a twenty-year-old black welfare mother of three, revealed that Dr. Pierce had demanded that she have her Fallopian tubes tied before he would deliver her third child. She agreed and was sterilized. Pondering and regretting her decision, Marietta Williams envisioned a bleak future for herself: "I wouldn't marry again. Who would want me, knowing I cannot have any children?"[6]

Dorothy Waters, a thirty-year-old black mother of five youngsters who is separated from her husband, has said that her sterilization was made possible by pressure and deceit. She has alleged that Dr. Pierce told her on the occasion of her final visit to his office that he would deliver her child only on the understanding that she be sterilized. Mrs. Waters has attributed the following remark to the doctor: "Listen here, young lady, this is my tax money paying for this baby and I'm tired of paying for illegitimate children." She demurred, whereupon he advised her to find another physician; however, because the baby was due any day, Mrs. Waters finally relented and was rendered sterile.[7]

Condemnation of coercive sterilization in Aiken County was

quick and to the point. "The actions of some in singling out mothers of three children who also receive welfare is totally irrelevant to the purposes of providing medical aid to the needy. This is contrary to the American concept of equality." So declared University of South Carolina law professor, Eldon Wedlock, president of South Carolina's American Civil Liberties Union affiliate.[8]

A $1.5 million lawsuit has been filed by the American Civil Liberties Union naming as defendants Dr. Pierce, the Aiken County Hospital, and two of its officials, the director of the Department of Social Services of Aiken County and the commissioner of the Department of Social Services of South Carolina. In order to protect their privacy and the privacy of their children, the two plaintiffs in this class action have not been identified. They are referred to by the fictitious names Jane Doe and Mary Roe. Both are residents of Aiken County; both are black.

The suit alleges that plaintiff Jane Doe, a twenty-four-year-old unmarried mother of four, prior to her last delivery, was informed by Dr. Pierce that unless she submitted to sterilization he would "refuse to attend her or her child during or after labor, would deny her access to Aiken County Hospital and . . . would see that her assistance from the Department of Social Services was terminated." Labor was imminent. The Department of Social Services declined to assist the plaintiff. In order to have her baby delivered under medical supervision, she gave her consent to be sterilized.

Plaintiff Mary Roe is the mother of three children, the last of whom was born in Aiken County Hospital in September 1973. The birth would make Mary Roe eligible for public assistance because childcare would necessitate her leaving her job. Medicaid would pay part of the obstetrician's fee. Mary Roe contends that Dr. Pierce informed her that "since she was going to receive assistance from the Department of Social Services and because she had three children she had to submit to involuntary sterilization and that if she refused she and her day old child would be summarily evicted and discharged from the hospital and that he would refuse to render her or her child post delivery care.'' The plaintiff rejected Dr. Pierce's ultimatum and claims that she was immediately expelled from the hospital.

Sterilization is obviously an extreme method of limiting fertility. Less drastic means of family planning were not adequately explored, the ACLU complaint charges. Nor were the coerced plaintiffs allowed freedom of choice so that they could select medical care and family planning aid compatible with the dictates of their consciences. Moreover, compulsion was applied to black persons on relief and not to whites or self-supporting persons.[9]

Most of the women affected by the obstetrical policy in Aiken County were penniless blacks. During the first six months of 1973 a total of eighteen welfare women were spayed. Seventeen of them were Afro-Americans. Would there have been an uproar had not a white woman, Carol Brown, publicized her experience?

Black commentary on the Aiken situation was predictably angry. The Black Panther party newspaper said that in actuality mothers with fewer than three children had been sterilized under what it called a ''fascist policy.'' Even black teenagers had been sterilized, one age fourteen, it charged. What the Panthers perceived was ''racist, genocidal extermination directed at poor Black girls and women.''[10]

The *Afro-American* editorially lambasted the ''master race theory'' which lay behind the Aiken brouhaha. To that respected, widely read black weekly, giving pregnant women a choice between undergoing sterilization or finding another hospital sounded like ''some sinister un-American horror story unravelling.''[11]

Not everyone saw things that way. There was substantial sympathy for Dr. Pierce and his philosophy in his own community. On the matter of sterilization the local ''silent majority'' was far from silent. Petitions were circulated on the physician's behalf shortly after national media coverage made the Aiken case a cause célèbre. One petition commented that for years welfare recipients had not taken advantage of free birth control which was available in the county. William R. Bland, a pharmacist and a prime mover in the petition drive, probably spoke for the thousands who affixed their signatures to the memorial, when he said that if he as a taxpayer was required to pay for relief recipients he would have a right to have a say in how they would be cared for. Bryan McCanless, executive director of the Chamber of Commerce, observed about welfare people, black and poor white "trash," who had babies that cost the taxpayer money: "I think everyone agrees they should be sterilized."[12] State representative Cecil Collins believed that the doctors had been too lenient. Were it up to him Collins would sterilize the welfare mother after her first out of wedlock birth.[13]

Also rallying to Dr. Pierce's aid was the Aiken County Medical Society. The society declared that it had not been *formally* [emphasis mine] advised of any wrongdoing nor of any complaint about the medical care rendered by Dr. Pierce. His medical colleagues proclaimed their wholehearted support and concern for Pierce. They attested to his "professional integrity and competence" and noted that he "has immeasurably contributed both quality and quantity care to all patients, be they self-supporting or indigent, and . . . proof of the same is available to anyone who might seek such information."[14]

As for the South Carolina Medical Association, its House of Delegates passed a motion in December 1973 asserting that a doctor shall be presumed innocent until such time as he has been formally accused and found guilty. Prior to conviction, the Medical Association would stand behind the physician in resisting any pressures brought against him by a third party.[15] Although Dr. Pierce's name was not mentioned, it was unquestionably the Aiken situation which gave rise to the motion. For its unswerving dedication to civil liberties and procedural due process, the South Carolina Medical Society deserves high praise. It is to be fervently hoped that the society will be equally zealous in protecting the rights of patients—poor, black patients in particular.

Amidst the furor that ensued over the Aiken sterilization scandal, several federal and state agencies launched investigations. In a press conference held on September 28, 1973, Dr. R. Archie Ellis, commissioner of the South Carolina State Board of Social

Services, summarized the actions to be taken following a probe conducted by his agency and that of the office of South Carolina's attorney general. Regarding the Pierce matter, on July 30, 1973, the Department of Health, Education and Welfare had apprised state officials that certain elements in the South Carolina plan for state medical assistance might be jeopardized by reason of reports which HEW had received concerning failure to comply with provisions of the plan relating to family planning. The plan stipulated that there should be freedom from coercion or pressure of mind and conscience, and that there ought to be freedom of choice of birth control method. Accordingly, the attorney general advised the State Department of Social Services to take corrective action to prevent a continuance or recurrence of the policies followed by Dr. Clovis Pierce in his treatment of patients in the Medicaid program. A letter was to be forwarded to Dr. Pierce warning him that bills for the delivery of babies would not be paid by the Department of Social Services unless he filed an affidavit attesting to his cessation of the objectionable, coercive sterilization practices which violated federal rules.[16]

Contributing more to the protest over sterilization than any other single incident was the sterilization of fourteen-year-old Minnie Lee Relf and her twelve-year-old sister Mary Alice Relf, the youngest of six children of a black Alabama couple. Both parents, Lonnie and Minnie Relf, are uneducated and illiterate, typical human "waste products" of agricultural automation and a deep-seated tradition of deprivation. Both had worked most of their lives as farmhands before relocating to a more urban setting. Their poverty was so severe at first that the family survived by garbage dump picking. Their fortunes appeared to brighten when they moved into public housing and, thanks to food stamps and welfare assistance, the Relfs managed to keep body and soul together. They were also able to avail themselves of the family planning services provided by a subdivision of the federally funded Montgomery Community Action Agency.

In June 1973 family planning nurses from the agency took Minnie Lee and Mary Alice from their home and had them admitted to the hospital. Their mother's story is that she was told that the girls would be given birth control inoculations. For some time contraceptive shots had been administered to them. A third daughter, Katie, age eighteen, who had previously been fitted with an intrauterine device after a miscarriage, supposedly averted sterilization by locking herself in a bedroom when the nurses came to fetch her.

Unable to read the consent form, Mrs. Relf was not knowingly authorizing the tubal ligations which were performed on her daughters after she scrawled her ''x'' on the dotted line. In July 1973 Senator Edward Kennedy's U.S. Senate Health Subcommittee held hearings on the sterilizations. Mrs. Relf told the committee that she did not learn that Minnie Lee and Mary Alice had actually had surgery until she went to visit her daughters in the hospital. By then the sterilizations were a fait accompli. ''I felt angry, didn't like it,'' Mrs. Relf stated. ''I wouldn't have let them done that.''[17] At the same Senate hearings Mr. Relf, who is now disabled, testified that he too did not discover what had happened until after the fact. Somewhat more alert than his wife, Lonnie Relf had not previously been contacted. Indeed, a lawyer for Mr. and Mrs. Relf stated that before the operation no physician ever spoke with any member of the family. Even after their experience the Relf sisters themselves did not understand the consequences of the operations they had undergone. Asked by one of her attorneys whether she intended to get married and have children, Minnie Lee Relf replied in the affirmative. She wanted to have a little girl.[18] Obviously, to avoid doing irreparable harm to innocent individuals, it is absolutely imperative that easily comprehensible information about methods, risks, and effects be imparted to persons contemplating sterilization or persons for whom sterilization is contemplated. In cases involving minor and/or retarded patients, it is critically important that that information be communicated to the parents or guardians.

Inevitably, the question of motive arises in connection with the Relf girls. What animated the Montgomery agency to ''fix'' the sisters as one would a pair of stray female cats? The search for

motives is ordinarily a frustrating and elusive task. That of the
family planners in Montgomery is no exception. Motivation
certainly cannot be pinpointed and verified. Mary Alice Relf may
be slightly retarded in her mental functioning, but tests have shown
her to be educable. Minnie Relf, however, is not even a borderline
case: her intelligence level is normal. Lawyers for the Relfs have
filed a one million dollar damage suit on their behalf. In their suit,
they score the agency officials for acting as self-appointed
protectors of the girls' morals and quote one nurse who said that
boys were "hanging around" the Relf home. Proof that either girl
was promiscuous or that either was guilty of moral turpitude has
never been presented.

Meanwhile, officials of the Montgomery Community Action
Agency and the director of the family planning clinic have firmly
denied any wrongdoing. They say that there was no misunderstanding, no breakdown in communications with Mrs. Relf.
They insist that the girls' mother had been counseled about the
surgery to be performed on the girls and that she had been briefed
about the anticipated result of the procedure—irreversible sterili-
ty. They claim that they decided on sterilization only after all
contraceptives had been found to be unfeasible. Further use of
Depo-Provera, the injectible, long-lasting anti-conception drug
which was being given to the Relf sisters, for example, had been
prohibited by the Department of Health, Education and Welfare
because research had suggested possible deleterious side effects.
Clinic personnel concluded that coils were not a suitable contraceptive substitute and that Minnie Lee and Mary Alice lacked
the discipline and mental capacity to take birth control pills on a
daily schedule.[19] By a process of elimination they hit upon tubal
ligation as the answer to the problem. Whether there really was a
problem is, of course, highly debatable.

Racism is suspected to be the true motive underlying the tube-
tying. All blacks—separatists and integrationists, radicals and
moderates alike—found the sterilization of the Relf youngsters
odious. "A blatant infringement on human rights," the *Chicago
Daily Defender* called it, and went on to say that it was "a clear

and revolting instance of Southern race prejudice intruding itself into the private lives of illiterate blacks bereft of either power or influence.''[20]

The blacks' outbursts of indignation were replete with references to genocide. The Black Panthers perceived growing evidence of an organized plot by the Montgomery Community Action organization and the Montgomery family planning center to sterilize black people in Alabama on a mass scale. In a strongly worded article entitled ''Genocide in Alabama,'' the Black Panther party newspaper said that the Montgomery sterilization amounted to the premeditated murder of a race. A subsequent issue of that publication tied the Relf scandal to the Tuskegee syphilis project and summed up by declaring that genocide had long been masked by medical science.[21]

To Lonnie Kashif of *Muhammad Speaks* the ordeal of the Relf girls was ''a deliberate act of genocidal sterilization.'' Black Muslims suggested that the Alabama tragedy was just the tip of the sterilization iceberg.[22]

Angrily denouncing the inhumane, willful, and malicious Montgomery sterilization was the Roanoke, Virginia, chapter of the National Association of Black Social Workers. Along with numberless other blacks, it suspected that the practice of pressured sterilization was more widespread than people realized.[23]

Julian Bond was nagged by the same suspicions. Was the Relf tragedy an isolated one, an aberration? Or had it happened before? In either case it ranked with the worst examples in history of ''inhumanity, insensitivity, callousness and cruelty.'' He called the deed ''this horrendous attack on privacy, on innocence, on the right to motherhood.'' Bond, president of the Southern Poverty Law Center which brought the lawsuit on the Relfs' behalf, told the press that the precedent for the sterilizations had been set by Nazi Germany.[24]

Expressing his views in the New York *Daily Challenge*, another one of the handful of black daily newspapers in the country, Charles E. Cob, executive director of the Commission for Racial Justice, wrote that the Montgomery sterilization ''regrettably demonstrates once again, the low esteem in which Black life is held and the genocidal nature of programs supposedly designed to help Blacks.''[25]

Black syndicated columnist William Raspberry observed that no "great rhetorical stretch" was required to call the tube-tying in question genocide. But, because the victims were always poor, perhaps "classicide" was more felicitous a term, Raspberry thought.[26]

Vernon Jordan, Jr., who succeeded the late Whitney Young as head of the Urban League, said of the sterilization that it was "an act that makes the blood run cold in its callous disregard for the most fundamental rights of the individual." Jordan also linked what had happened in Montgomery with that other moral catastrophe in Alabama, the Tuskegee syphilis project. The menace of "racial extermination" was present whether recognizable as such or not. It was no coincidence that the target population was Afro-American. Sterilization of the retarded was but the first step just as it had been with the Nazis. Immoral individuals, welfare mothers of illegitimate children, would be next. After them, Jordan warned, will come "some racial group or identifiable caste that is open for punishment, for experimentation, or, finally, for genocidal measures."[27]

Among the most concerned and articulate voices raised in the whole sterilization controversy were those belonging to four black congresswomen: Yvonne Burke, Democrat of California; Shirley Chisholm, Democrat of New York; Cardiss Collins, Democrat of Illinois; and Barbara Jordan, Democrat of Texas. Although they were acutely aware of the gravity of the sterilization dispute, the congresswomen refused to be carried away by the genocide talk. The heart of the matter, they wrote to HEW Secretary Caspar Weinberger on July 10, 1973, was how to make "family planning information and services availableso those individuals who want and need them and at the same time insure that no element of coercion creeps into programs which Congress has *specifically* mandated must be voluntary in nature." The congresswomen reminded Secretary Weinberger that a few years earlier birth control information would not have been granted public assistance recipients, even "if they got down on their knees and begged for it." But now, some social workers were so avid as to be "pushy." Information and aid ought to be provided, not imposed, a difference which was central to the whole birth control debate.[28]

The four representatives prodded HEW to develop clear and consistent sterilization guidelines. They advocated the creation of a review panel which would reflect the kind of women being served in minority communities. This would help combat the foreboding in these communities "that sterilization and other methods of birth control could be abused if the rights of the patient are not vigilantly maintained." If minority group women had a say in policy- and decision-making, and if patient rights were safeguarded, then the Montgomery and Aiken County cases and the spectre of "race genocide" which they conjured up would be banished.[29] Events in Aiken County had revealed to Representatives Burke, Chisholm, Collins, and Jordan just what could take place if a doctor was allowed "to play God."

The congresswomen, aware of the propensity of some physicians for self-deification, were sensitive about possible abuses connected with Depo-Provera, the experimental contraceptive that had been used on the Relf girls. In October 1973 the Food and Drug Administration had given only limited approval to the anti-conception drug because there was some evidence that it increased the risk of embolisms, breast cancer, and infertility. Would the use of Depo-Provera be restricted to minority poor and mentally retarded women? The FDA was advising doctors that the drug was to be prescribed under limited circumstances, such as when the patient "is incapable or unwilling to tolerate the side effects of conventional oral contraceptives," or "refuses or is unable to accept the responsibility demanded by other contraceptive methods." Did this advice reflect the FDA's desire to confine Depo-Provera to people like the Relfs? The congresswomen thought so.

In a civil action, *Relf* v. *Weinberger*, a major complaint was that Depo-Provera had been administered to the three Relf girls without their informed consent or that of their parents. "This intrusion into the plaintiffs' bodies and personal lives," the suit charged, was an invasion of basic constitutional rights.[30] Harmless, approved alternatives to Depo-Provera were available. Therefore, a motion was made asking the court to bar the use of experimental birth control drugs pending the drawing up of adequate protective guidelines.

Among the many tangled issues raised by the Relf case were the rights of minors and those of the mentally retarded in regard to their sexual autonomy. Largely in response to the Relf sterilizations, some fourteen organizations led by the National Council of Negro Women, and including ZPG, jointly asked that the use of federal moneys for the sterilization of minors be terminated. It was plain to those requesting the policy change that "neither Federal nor state law and regulations took adequate cognizance of the difficult issues involved where the sterilization of minors is to be considered and of the potential for abuse, especially when dealing with individuals who are particularly vulnerable because of age."[31] Attorneys for the Relfs had asked the courts to halt sterilization—an irreversible birth control procedure—on minors whose rights, after all, corresponded to those of adults.[32] They further suggested that the courts prohibit the sterilization of mental incompetents. They even wanted to bar the sterilization of competent adults because the obligatory sterilizations in Aiken and elsewhere cast serious doubts on whether requests were made freely and without pressure.

In March 1974 Judge Gerhard Gesell of the United States District Court for the District of Columbia found that the secretary of HEW had no statutory authority to "fund the sterilization of persons incompetent under state law to consent to an operation whether because of minority or mental deficiency." HEW regulations were found to be unreasonable and arbitrary inasmuch as they did not comply with the congressional mandate that federal family planning money not be utilized to pressure poor patients into sterilization. Family planning sterilizations assisted by the federal government, Judge Gesell ruled, were allowable only with the "voluntary, knowing and uncoerced consent of individuals competent to give such consent." Before consent is solicited, the person must be given to understand that, should he or she decline to be sterilized, no benefits provided by programs receiving federal funds will be withdrawn or withheld. Judge Gesell ordered that the sterilization regulations be modified to conform with the court's decision.[33]

What of the federal guidelines already in existence to protect the rights of individuals undergoing sterilization operations? Why did they not protect the Relf youngsters? Somehow the guidelines had been lost or *misplaced* in the bureaucratic labyrinth. In the wake of the Relf scandal, it was discovered that cartons containing twenty-five thousand copies of the guidelines had been sitting on shelves gathering dust in government warehouses. Those guidelines had been ably prepared by the family planning division of the Office of Economic Opportunity in 1971 when a policy change made possible for the first time the use of anti-poverty funds for sterilization purposes. Previously, operative OEO regulations had explicitly barred the expenditure of project funds for sterilization procedures. Voluntarism was a guiding principle of the guidelines. Force and pressure were specifically forbidden. Patients had to request the operation. In addition, they had to be persons who possessed the legal capacity to give consent and who appreciated the attendant risks and possible repercussions.

But the rather detailed guidelines were never implemented or, for that matter, distributed. Why? One explanation has come from Dr. E. Leon Cooper, a black pediatrician who in November 1971 became director of Health Affairs in OEO. He has cited budgetary considerations and program priorities. Another factor was that OEO was having difficulties with a pilot project in Anderson County, Tennessee. Concerns about coercion and confidentiality related to sterilization were supposedly at the root of the difficulties, says Dr. Cooper, who also states that he was personally responsible for holding back the guidelines from circulation.

An alternative version, perhaps equally plausible, is that the guidelines were suppressed, largely for political reasons. With the

1972 elections in the offing, the White House may have been loath to permit OEO funds to be used for sterilization, lest conservative support, especially Catholic support, be lost.[34]

Which version is correct? We cannot say with any certainty. Nor can we know for sure if dissemination and implementation of the guidelines would have averted the Relf disaster. Clio, the muse of history, never responds to the always fascinating "if" questions. We can only wonder.

## NOTES

1. This information has been drawn from the preliminary brief filed by the plaintiff in the United States District Court for the Eastern District of North Carolina, Washington Division in *Cox* v. *Stanton et al.*, and from an ACLU news release (undated).

2. *Amsterdam News*, 21 July 1973.

3. Ibid.

4. Amended Complaint filed in the United States District Court for the Western District of Pennsylvania in *Serena* v. *Leezer*, No. 74-313.

5. *Afro-American*, 28 July 1973, and *New York Times*, 28 July 1973.

6. *New York Times*, 1 August 1973.

7. *Washington Post*, 24 July 1973.

8. Emily Bull, "ACLU Planning to File Sterilization Lawsuit," *Aiken Standard*, 15 April 1974.

9. Complaint filed in the United States District Court for the District of South Carolina, Aiken Division in *Doe and Roe* v. *Pierce et al.*, No. 74-475.

10. *The Black Panther*, 11 August 1973.

11. *Afro-American*, 28 July 1973.

12. Ibid., 11 August 1973.

13. Henry Leifermann, "They Still Think Sterilization Is Good Enough for Welfare Mothers," *Southern Voices* 1, No. 2 (May-June 1974): 80.

14. News release from the Aiken County Medical Society quoting a resolution passed by that body on 1 October 1973 and reaffirmed on 6 May 1974.

15. Position paper adopted by the South Carolina Medical Association, 23 April 1974.

16.  Statement by Dr. R. Archie Ellis made at a press conference on 28 September 1973.

17.  *Afro-American*, 21 July 1973.

18.  B. Drummond Ayres, "Sterilizing the Poor—Exploring Motives and Methods," *New York Times*, "News of the Week in Review," 8 July 1973.

19.  Ibid.

20.  *Chicago Daily Defender*, 25 July 1973.

21.  *The Black Panther*, 7 July 1973, and 14 July 1973.

22.  *Muhammad Speaks*, 13 July 1973, and 27 July 1973.

23.  See letter by James A. Williams of Roanoke, Virginia, chapter of the National Association of Black Social Workers to *Roanoke, Virginia Times*, 22 July 1973.

24.  Daryl Alexander, "A Montgomery Tragedy." *Essence*, September 1973, p. 43 and the *Afro-American*, 7 July 1973.

25.  *Daily Challenge*, 17 July 1973.

26.  William Raspberry, "Classicide—Sterilization Is the New Social Work," *Philadelphia Inquirer*, 27 July 1973.

27.  Vernon Jordan, Jr., "To Be Equal—Sterilization Scandal Shows Experimenters Still Busy," *Afro-American*, 28 July 1973.

28.  Congresswomen Yvonne Burke, Shirley Chisholm, Cardiss Collins, Barbara Jordan, letter to HEW Secretary Caspar W. Weinberger, 10 July 1973.

29.  Joint Press Release, 22 October 1973.

30.  Plaintiff's Brief in Support of Motion for Preliminary Injunction Filed in the United States District Court for the District of Columbia in *Katie Relf et al.* v. *Weinberger et al.*, Civil Action No. 73-1557.

31.  *New York Times*, 10 July 1973.

32.  Plaintiff's Brief, *Relf* v. *Weinberger*.

33.  Memorandum Opinion in the United States District Court for the District of Columbia in *Relf* v. *Weinberger*, Civil Action No. 73-1557, and *National Welfare Rights Organization* v. *Weinberger*, Civil Action No. 74-243. These two related cases were consolidated to challenge HEW regulations governing sterilization.

34.  See "Sterilization Guidelines: 22 Months on the Shelf," *Medical World News*, 9 November 1973, pp. 53 ff., for a detailed analysis of this bureaucratic snafu.

# 12 . *Concluding Thoughts*

In response to white racist brutality over the centuries blacks have evolved antennae highly sensitive to potential dangers. In a Darwinian sense these acute antennae could have survival value should genocide, the ultimate danger, become a reality. Just how real is the threat of genocide? Perhaps a more important question is "How real do blacks think the genocidal peril is?"

That most rapid and efficient disseminator of information in the black community, Dame Rumor, periodically transmits word of a government-sponsored plot to deal ruthlessly with black unrest. In the late 1960s there was scuttlebutt about a plan to intern black youth in detention camps before they could develop violent and radical inclinations.[1] Black community grapevines also spoke of the so-called King Alfred Plan to counteract the rising tide of black militancy. Documents purported to be part of the scheme revealed that government planners believed racial war would inevitably follow attempts to stymy the black thrust for equal justice. "When that emergency comes," the document reads, "we must expect the total involvement of all 22 million members of the Minority, men, women, and children, for once the project is launched, its goal is to terminate, once and for all, the Minority threat to the whole of the American society and, indeed the Free World." These ominous words were quoted in a recent article on genocide and population control published in *The Black Scholar.*[2] They appeared first in *The Man Who Cried I Am*, a novel by the gifted black author, John A. Williams. In Williams' version of the King Alfred Plan, minority members would be evacuated from the cities and detained in military installations and minority members of Congress would be unseated. Black organizations and leaders were already under surveillance around the clock.[3]

The King Alfred Plan is probably wholly spurious, for no proof of its authenticity has been produced. Williams has candidly stated that his King Alfred Plan was "a fiction based upon a history that could be cast into the future."[4] Is Williams an alarmist? Anticipation of ghetto-based guerrilla warfare in 1968 following the assassination of Martin Luther King, Jr., prompted the House Un-American Activities Committee to draw up contingency plans which were then recommended to President Lyndon B. Johnson. The ghetto would be sealed off. A curfew would be imposed at sundown and most civil liberties would be suspended. Individuals found with weapons would be arrested as would persons without proper identification. Warring guerrillas, the committee suggested, could be interned in the detention centers provided for by the McCarran Act.[5]

Copies of Department of Justice memoranda recently made public tend to confirm black fears of governmental antipathy to the cause of racial justice. In one directive, J. Edgar Hoover, the late Director of the Federal Bureau of Investigation, in effect, ordered FBI offices to subvert the civil rights movement. Specifically, he wanted his staff to undermine black coalitions and to block the rise of a black "messiah" around whom black groups could unite. Neutralization of black nationalists in particular was the goal of another Hoover memo.[6] Attorney General William Saxbe acknowledged that the FBI under Hoover's direction conducted counter-intelligence operations against subversive, violence-prone groups. Among the targets of the FBI's disruptive activities were the Student Nonviolent Coordinating Committee, the Congress of Racial Equality, and significantly, Martin Luther King's Southern Christian Leadership Conference, an organization whose name has been synonymous with nonviolence. These facts together with Hoover's surveillance and harassment of Dr. King, lead to the inescapable conclusion that he was hostile to black civil rights leadership regardless of ideology.

"Subversive," "radical" groups were also closely watched by the Internal Revenue Service at the behest of the despotic Nixon White House. Included in its surveillance list were the Black Panther party and the Nation of Islam as well as several other black separatist and militant groups. Also suspect were the Welfare Rights Organization and even the Urban League, which is hardly a radical enterprise.[7] What all of this means is that one need not suffer from delusions of persecution to think aloud, "Is the King Alfred Plan so unthinkable?" For that matter, genocide of blacks is not completely unthinkable in the future. True, it is a possibility rather than a probability, but their collective experience has shown that blacks have good reason to be constantly watchful.

What of birth control in particular? Should blacks be wary of it? In the first chapter of this book, specific questions were posed about the rationality of black fears of birth control as a genocidal tool of the white man. From the evidence available it is fair to conclude that contraception, abortion, and sterilization have never been systematically used to exterminate black Americans. There has never been a genocidal master plan, but there is much in the historical record and in contemporary societal developments to sustain black fears about the existence of such a plan. Blacks and other minorities need to be vigilant if birth control, a great blessing, is not to be misused to their detriment.

We have seen how black sexuality has been trifled with and manipulated by white Americans ever since Africans were first imported as cargo. A long train of sexual abuses—slave breeding, rape of female slaves by their masters, legalized punitive castration, and sexual mutilation of lynch victims—has made black "paranoia" especially severe in the sexual sector of human behavior. Herein lies one of the several wellsprings of black apprehension of white efforts to put fertility-limiting methods at their disposal.

Another wellspring has been the *volte-face* by federal, state, and city governments on the issue of family planning. Birth control services, long anathema to politicians, are now government-subsidized. Today's elected officials are more enlightened than their predecessors, but this does not truly explain government endorsement of planned parenthood. Ever increasing public assistance expenditures have convinced many a politico that family planning is a necessity to combat the welfare monster. Because governments appear to give high priority to making birth control information and devices accessible to the indigent while the jobs, housing, and medical care much needed by blacks are put on back burners, black anxiety about birth control is nourished.

That anxiety can easily be transformed into paranoia. Blacks tend to walk a thin line of paranoia, Julian Bond has opined. The symptoms can be unfortunate. For example, the Black Muslims and other blacks, usually males, have interpreted the legalization of abortion as genocidal because most of those who take advantage of opportunities opened up by the new legal statutes are impoverished black women. A more rational analysis, the one frequently made by black spokeswomen, is that the removal of abortion from the criminal code constitutes a long overdue social reform, that it spells finis to hypocritical double standards that made safe abortions possible for the affluent but consigned poor pregnant black females to backstreet underworld butchers.

Punitive sterilization bills aimed at welfare mothers are another source of the genocide idea. None has ever been enacted into law but these bills feed black paranoia nonetheless. They are a frightening reminder of what some whites would like to bring about.

A large segment of the American public equates the welfare problem with the presence of Afro-Americans. Indolent, sexually promiscuous black welfare mothers and their illegitimate offspring are held responsible for the tax burden which weighs so heavily on middle-class America's shoulders. Other enormous budgetary items, defense for example, are overlooked, as is the fact that for two and a half centuries black slaves worked without compensation. Overlooked too is the racial discrimination in education and employment which is the root cause of our monumental welfare problem.

It is common "knowledge" that public assistance provides an incentive to the welfare mother to be reproductively prolific. The more children she has, the more substantial her welfare check. True enough, but normally the payments are sufficient to meet only the minimal needs of the family. Moreover, in a majority of the states progressively smaller amounts are paid for each additional child. And in 1972 40 percent of the states had ceilings on payments to families regardless of their size.[8]

Underlying punitive sterilization bills is deep misunderstanding about welfare. But debunking welfare mythology is about as easy as unscrambling eggs.

Black and white allies who deplore the infringement of sexual and contraceptive freedom have reacted strongly to coercive sterilization. In 1973 at a time when five states were contemplating legislation that would have forced or enticed public assistance recipients to undergo surgical sterilization, a joint statement was issued by the predominantly black one hundred twenty-five thousand member National Welfare Rights Organization and the Association for Voluntary Sterilization. Mrs. Johnnie Tillman, executive director of the National Welfare Rights Organization, and Dr. Charles T. Faneuff, executive director of the Association for Voluntary Sterilization, opposed passage of the five bills, saying that, "Compulsory sterilization is a violation of inalienable human rights and an unreasonable assault on human dignity." Both concurred with a resolution adopted by the ACLU which declared that "the whole question of human reproduction should be a matter of voluntary decision with no governmental compulsion. The right to practice any birth control procedures by either women or men, including contraception, abortion and sterilization, should be an individual's decision, and no compulsion or coercion can be tolerated."[9]

Forcible sterilization of the Relf adolescents in Alabama and the involuntary sterilizations in Aiken County, South Carolina, show that blacks must be on their guard even if punitive legislation is not enacted. There is no need for a genocidal plot to be hatched in the Oval Office or Congressional cloakrooms. Verified abuses, coupled with unverifiable community gossip about women duped or pressured into sterilization, are enough to fire the black imagination.

Population has become an increasingly controversial topic in the 1960s and the 1970s, owing in large measure to the zero population movement. Foresighted individuals worried about the deleterious effects of continued unchecked population growth were the driving force behind the movement. On the global level, too many people would mean massive famine, especially in developing areas, ZPG proponents predicted. On the national level, too many people would mean a deterioration in the quality of life. In addition, if the United States did not adopt a population control policy it would hardly be in a position to effectively preach about the virtues of limited population growth. After all, because of our high standard of living, the average American's consumption of nonrenewable resources is many times greater than that of an inhabitant of a much poorer country. Zero population growth enthusiasts rightly urged Americans to limit their families voluntarily to two children each in the hope of stabilizing population. But in so doing they have raised the spectre of possible governmental interference in what have been personal decisions about family size, should voluntarism fail. A small minority of ZPG zealots who see the population situation as one that is already grave have advocated coercion to reduce fertility. To blacks and other vulnerable Americans the prospect of coercion is frightening.

In this connection it is crucial to remember that the lower classes, including nonwhite minorities, are not the principal culprits in our slow but steady population growth. Writing in 1971 Paul Ehrlich and John P. Holdren noted that under one-third of the babies born annually in the United States are born to poor families. Less than one of five newborn infants are born to nonwhites. Self-supporting, middle-class Americans who can afford that third or fourth or fifth child are the real offenders.[10] If black and

Hispanic parents had produced no children at all throughout the 1960s, the population of the United States at the end of the decade would have been only 4 percent smaller.[11] Contrary to popular wisdom, welfare families are not significantly larger than self-supporting families—just one-half child bigger on the average.[12] "The idea that our population growth is primarily fueled by the poor and minorities having lots of babies is a myth," the Population Commission declared unequivocally in 1972.[13]

Many black pro-natalists believe that having lots of babies is the best solution to their racial dilemma, a numerical antidote to discrimination, a kind of insurance against liquidation. For decades this strength-in-numbers philosophy, so common among ethnic, racial, and national groups, has been one of the main underpinnings of the black genocide ideology. In contrast to most integrationist civil rights advocates, beginning with W. E. B. DuBois who preferred birth control to "death control" (a high death rate) and who emphasized the quality, not the quantity, of the black populace, many black Americans have espoused the idea that by becoming a larger percentage of the American people blacks will gain more power. In my judgment even a sharp increase in the proportion of Americans of African descent would not guarantee an enhancement of black power. It would not, in all likelihood, presage an improvement in black living conditions. The reverse would probably occur. Helter-skelter black propagation for political purposes is a callous, misguided strategy.

This study has dealt primarily with the public utterances and writings of black American opinion makers. Between their pronouncements on birth control and the practice of contraception by millions of Afro-Americans there may be a sizable gap. There is a large body of evidence suggesting that the black masses are no more responsive to the genocide notion than American Catholics are to papal encyclicals on artificial contraception. In a study published in 1970, Donald Bogue found that 80 percent of his Chicago sample of black women ghetto dwellers approved of birth control and 75 percent were actually practicing it. Bogue thought it "possible that the controversy over birth control for Negroes has eroded approval of family planning somewhat although it is still overwhelmingly positive.''[14] A recent opinion study revealed that a significant majority of blacks want the government to provide contraceptive information and supplies, want the government to make abortion available to all women, and desire the legalization of sterilization operations.[15]

Using Census Bureau data, demographer James A. Sweet of the University of Wisconsin has marked some important differentials in the rate of fertility decline in the United States from 1960 to 1970. Fertility has actually been dropping since 1957. While the fertility of urban white married females dropped by 26.8 percent from the triennium 1957-1960 to the triennium 1967-1970, the fertility rate for blacks as a whole plummeted by 36.8 percent. In 1957-1960 the rate for blacks was 24 percent higher than that for urban whites, but in 1967-1970 it was only 7 percent higher. Fertility rates for southern rural blacks, southern urban blacks, and nonsouthern blacks all fell sharply by more than one-third to a point where they were below that for urban whites ten years earlier. In sum, the American birth rate has been appreciably reduced. The traditionally higher rate for poor Americans has been slashed even more sharply.[16] Poor nonwhite birth rates have shown the steepest decline. Impecunious Americans are still significantly more fruitful than their economic betters and blacks still have more children than whites, but the birth gap is being closed. One implication of these dramatic changes noted by Sweet is that a smaller share of American children "will be growing up in impoverished settings with large numbers of siblings present in the family. If this is the case, whatever long-term impact poverty and large numbers of siblings may have on life chances should be substantially diminished.''[17]

Organized family planning programs, many of them federally subsidized, help to explain the foregoing demographic phenomenon. Poor women, including blacks, have made excellent use of birth control clinics. From 1967 to 1973 there was a fivefold jump in the number of women taking advantage of family planning facilities. In excess of 3.2 million women were benefiting from the

programs offered by health departments, hospitals, and affiliates
of Planned Parenthood. Eighty-five percent of those women were
drawn from low or marginal income families. By introducing
them—many of whom had previously not been using contraceptives—to the most effective birth control methods, poor
females have been given the same safeguards against unwanted
pregnancy that their more affluent sisters have had.[18]

Nevertheless, unwanted fertility rates for indigent classes continue to run well above those for women in higher income
brackets. For the period 1966 to 1970, 27 percent of black
childbearing was unwanted. Sixty-one percent was unplanned.
This compared with 13 percent unwanted childbearing among
white women, who also reported that 42 percent of their births
were unplanned.[19]

It was estimated in 1974 that approximately 9.2 million
American women in straitened circumstances still required
planned parenthood services to avert unwanted pregnancy.[20] A
substantial number are Americans of African descent. Teenage
illegitimacy, most of it unwanted, is dramatically higher for black
girls than for white girls. For those blacks the genocide rhetoric or
any agitational propaganda which inhibits the spread of family
planning services is disastrous.

Of course, the presence or absence of contraceptive facilities is
not the sole determinant of how many children black women bear.
Economic and social justice are pivotal. People must be motivated
to want fewer children. They must be motivated to practice contraception. As matters stand now, many of the indigent are
engulfed by despair. Their aspirations and ambitions are severely
circumscribed, if not extinguished altogether. Under such conditions having another child may be the only act of creativity they
can perform, the only means by which they can trumpet the
humanity which society denies them.

As new opportunities for personal advancement materialize, as
more and more black Americans and other oppressed minorities
elevate themselves to the middle classes, family size preferences
will surely be lowered. This is one of the important lessons

demographic history has to teach. So the sooner we upgrade housing, the quicker we provide quality education and gainful employment to those on the lowest rungs of the social ladder, the more receptive they will be to the idea of smaller families.

It is not my intention to minimize family planning —far from it. But neither the acceptance or rejection of family planning, nor the acceptance or rejection of the genocide thesis, is separable from the overall status of blacks in white America.

What can we expect in the future? There may be a dark cloud or two on the horizon. Data from a New England pilot project carried out in Hartford, Connecticut, in 1970 indicated that black males under thirty were more likely to concur with the genocide conspiracy theory and were much more hesitant about condoning limitations of black family size than were older black males.[21]

Age was a critical factor in a second study which was carried out in Philadelphia and Charlotte, North Carolina. The study revealed that younger blacks were more fearful of genocide accomplished by family planning than were older blacks. Black males had greater misgivings than black females and the northern sample was more anxious than the southern one. Subjects with less formal education expressed fear more than subjects with more schooling.[22]

An examination of family planning attitudes in California convinced investigators that black students had strong views about "honkie"-devised machinations to kill Afro-Americans. They sensed that a "War on People" would be aimed at them and their brothers.[23]

Whether such feelings will be acted upon, that is, matched by fertility behavior, remains to be seen. It may be surmised that black women who will have to bear and raise black children are not likely to be interested in abstract political and philosophical questions. Data from the New England study confirm this. Nevertheless, genocide polemics will surely continue to be heard, for black "paranoia" is anchored in historical reality. The black people's qualms about birth control may be partially dissipated by inviting black community involvement in birth control projects, by integrating family planning into comprehensive health care programs, by utilizing black personnel wherever possible. But until America solves the manifold problems of seething cauldrons which are our black ghettos, until blacks cease to be an exploited underclass, until black Americans obtain the power to shape their own destinies, indeed, until the nightmare of racism and oppression is supplanted for all by the American dream, until then it is unlikely that the genocide rhetoric will be muted.

## NOTES

1. Ronald Walters, "Population Control and the Black Community," Part I, *The Black Scholar* 5, No. 8 (May 1974): 49.

2. Ibid.

3. John A. Williams, *The Man Who Cried I Am* (Boston: Little, Brown and Co., 1967), pp. 371-375.

4. John A. Williams, letter to the author, 19 August 1974.

5. *Guerrilla Warfare Advocates in the United States.* Report by the Committee on Un-American Activities, House of Representatives, 19th Congress, 2d Session (Washington, D.C.: U.S. Government Printing Office, 1968), pp. 58-59.

6. *New York Times*, 6 April 1974. The memos were dated 25 April 1967 and 4 March 1968.

7. Ibid., 18 and 19 November 1974.

8. *Population and the American Future—The Report of the Commission on Population Growth and the American Future* (New York: New American Library, 1972), p. 158.

9. Association for Voluntary Sterilization press release, 18 June 1973.

10. Paul R. Ehrlich and John P. Holdren, "Who Makes the Babies?" *Saturday Review*, 6 February 1971, p. 60.

11. *Population and the American Future*, p. 109.

12. Ibid., p. 158.

13. Ibid., p. 109.

14. Donald J. Bogue, "Family Planning in the Negro Ghettos of Chicago," *Milbank Memorial Fund Quarterly* No. 2 (April 1970), Part 2: 283-299.

15. Gerald Lipson and Dianne Wolman, "Polling Americans on Birth Control and Population," *Family Planning Perspectives* 4 (January 1972): 39-42.

16. James A. Sweet, "Differentials in the Rate of Fertility Decline: 1960-1970," *Family Planning Perspectives* 6 (Spring 1974): 104-105.

17. Ibid., p. 107. On the other hand, rapidly falling black fertility will be used to validate the genocide theory. But if genocide is defined literally to mean the total extinction of the black race in the United States, then, according to the projections of one demographer, Ernest Attah, the period of extinction would exceed six thousand years. Because of the millennia involved during which the pattern of racial demise would surely be discerned and could be resisted, "the encouragement of fertility limitation among the black population—even to levels far below current levels among the white population—may be discounted as a viable instrument of genocide." Ernest B. Attah, "Racial Aspects of Zero Population Growth: Some Perspectives With Demographic Models." Paper prepared for presentation to the Population Association of America, April 1972.

18. Marsha Corey, "The State of Organized Family Planning Programs in the United States, 1973," *Family Planning Perspectives* 6, No. 1 (Winter 1974): 15, 19-20.

19. *Population and the American Future*, p. 164.

20. Planning Unit. Center for Family Planning Program Development, "The Need for Family Planning Services in the United States, 1974," *Family Planning Perspectives* 6, No. 1 (Winter 1974): 27.

21. William A. Darity, Castellano B. Turner, and H. Jean Thiebaux, "Race Consciousness and Fears of Black Genocide As Barriers to Family Planning." Paper presented at the Ninth Annual Meeting of the American Association of Planned Parenthood Physicians, Kansas City, Mo., 5 and 6 April 1971.

22. Castellano B. Turner and William A. Darity, "Fears of Genocide Among Black Americans As Related to Age, Sex, and Region," *American Journal of Public Health* 63, No. 12 (December 1973): 1034.

23. Robert Buckhout, "Toward a Two-Child Norm: Changing Family Planning Attitudes," *American Psychologist* 27 (1972): 23.

# Bibliography

## BOOKS, PAMPHLETS, AND MONOGRAPHS

Anonymous, and Jones, Thomas H. *The Experience of Thomas H. Jones Who Was a Slave for Forty-Three Years.* New Bedford: E. Anthony and Sons, 1871.

Bancroft, Frederick. *'Slave-Trading in the Old South.* Baltimore: J. H. Furst Co., 1931.

Baraka, Imamu Amiri (ed.). *African Congress—A Documentary of the First Modern Pan-African Congress.* New York: William Morrow, 1972.

Barrett, Leonard E. *The Rastafarians—A Study in Messianic Cultism in Jamaica.* Rio Piedras: Institute of Caribbean Studies, 1968.

Ben-Gurion, David. *Israel—A Personal History.* New York: Funk and Wagnalls, Inc., 1971.

*Better Health for 13,000,000.* New York: Planned Parenthood Federation of America, 1943.

Bibb, Henry. *Narrative of the Life and Times of Henry Bibb, An American Slave.* New York: Published by the Author, 1850.

Billingsley, Andrew. *Black Families in White America.* Englewood Cliffs, N.J.: Prentice-Hall, Inc., 1968.

Blake, Margaret Jane. *Memoirs of Margaret Jane Blake of Baltimore, Maryland.* Philadelphia: Press of Innes and Son, 1897.

Bleuel, Hans Peter. *Sex and Society in Nazi Germany.* Trans. J. Maxwell Brownjohn. Philadelphia: J. B. Lippincott Co., 1973.

Boston Women's Health Book Collective. *Our Bodies Ourselves—A Book by and for Women.* New York: Simon and Schuster, 1973.

Botkin, B. A. *Lay My Burden Down—A Folk History of Slavery.* Chicago: University of Chicago Press, 1958.

Bouvier, Leon F., and Lee, Everett S. *Black America.* Population Profiles. No. 10 (Washington, Conn.: Center for Information on America, 1974).

Brown, H. Rap. *Die Nigger Die.* New York: The Dial Press, 1969.

Byron, David, and Cole, Steven G. *A Sourcebook of Vasectomy.* Behavioral Science Monograph Series #72-1. Texas Christian University Press, June 1972.

Chisholm, Shirley. *Unbought and Unbossed.* New York: Avon Books, 1971.

Consuegra, José. *El Control de la Natalidad Como Arma del Imperialismo.* Buenos Aires: Editorial Galerna, 1969.

Cronon, E. David. *Black Moses: The Story of Marcus Garvey and the Universal Negro Improvement Association.* Madison: University of Wisconsin Press, 1969.

Curtin, Philip D. *The Atlantic Slave Trade—A Census.* Madison: University of Wisconsin Press, 1969.

"Demographic Aspects of the Black Community." *Proceedings of the Forty-Third Conference of the Milbank Memorial Fund.* Edited by Clyde V. Kiser. *Milbank Memorial Fund Quarterly* 48, No. 2 (April 1970), Part II.

Douglass, Frederick. *Life and Times of Frederick Douglass.* Hartford: Park Publishing Co., 1882.

DuBois, Victor D. *Population Review 1970: Ivory Coast.* American Universities Field Staff Reports, West Africa Series XIII, No. 1, 1971.

Ehrlich, Paul R. *The Population Bomb.* New York: Ballantine Books, 1968.

Essien-Udom, E. U. *Black Nationalism—A Search for an Identity in America.* New York: Dell Publishing Co., 1964.

Farley, Reynolds. *Growth of the Black Population: A Study of Demographic Trends.* Chicago: Markham Publishing Co., 1970.

Feldstein, Stanley. *Once a Slave—The Slave's View of Slavery.* New York: William Morrow and Co., Inc. 1971.

Fire, John/Lame Deer and Erdoes, Richard. *Lame Deer—Seeker of Visions.* New York: Simon and Schuster, 1972.

Flanders, Ralph Betts. *Plantation Slavery in Georgia.* Cos Cob, Conn.: John E. Edwards, Publisher, 1967.

Fogel, Robert William, and Engerman, Stanley L. *Time on the Cross—The Economics of American Negro Slavery.* Boston: Little, Brown and Co., 1974.

Foner, Philip S. (ed.). *The Black Panthers Speak.* Philadelphia: J. B. Lippincott Co., 1970.

Frazier, E. Franklin. *The Negro Family in the United States.* Chicago: University of Chicago Press, 1939.

Gallagher, Charles F. "The United Nations System and Population Problems." American Universities Field Staff Reports, Vol. 5, No. 5 (April 1970).

Garvey, Marcus. *Philosophy and Opinions of Marcus Garvey.* Edited by Amy Jacques Garvey. London: Frank Cass and Co. Ltd., 1967.

*Genocide in Mississippi.* Atlanta: The Student Nonviolent Coordinating Committee, n.d.

Goodell, William. *The American Slave Code in Theory and Practice.* New York: The New American Library, 1969.

Gregory, Dick. *Write Me In.* New York: Bantam Books, 1968.

Grünberger, Richard. *The 12 Year Reich— A Social History of Nazi Germany.* New York: Holt, Rinehart and Winston, 1971

*Guerrilla Warfare Advocates in the United States.* Report by the Committee on Un-American Activities, House of Representatives, 19th Congress, 2d Session, Washington, D.C.: U.S. Government Printing Office, 1968.

*Hearings Before the Sub-Committee on Health of the Committee on Labor and Public Welfare.* United States Senate, 93d Congress, 1st Session on S 974, 7 and 8 March 1973, Part 3. Washington, D.C.: U.S. Government Printing Office, 1973.

Himes, Norman E. *Medical History of Contraception.* Baltimore: The Williams and Wilkins Co., 1936.

Hooker, James R. *Population Planning in Rhodesia, 1971.* American Universities Field Staff Reports, Central and Southern Africa Series XV, No. 6. (1971).

———*Population Review 1970: Malawi.* American Universities Field Staff Reports, Central and Southern Africa Series XV, No. 1 (1971).

Jacobs, Harriet (Brent). *Incidents in the Life of a Slave Girl.* Edited by L. Maria Child. Boston: Published for the Author, 1861.

Jordan, Winthrop D. *The White Man's Burden—Historical Origins of Racism in the United States*. London: Oxford University Press, 1974.

———*White Over Black— American Attitudes Toward the Negro 1550-1812*. Chapel Hill: University of North Carolina Press, 1968.

Kennedy, David M. *Birth Control in America—The Career of Margaret Sanger*. New Haven and London: Yale University Press, 1970.

King, Martin Luther, Jr. *Family Planning—A Special and Urgent Concern*. New York: Planned Parenthood—World Population, n.d.

Kirkpatrick, Clifford. *Nazi Germany: Its Women and Family Life*. Indianapolis: The Bobbs-Merrill Co., 1938.

Ladner, Joyce A. *Tommorow's Tomorrow—The Black Woman*. Garden City, N. Y.: Anchor Books, 1972.

Lerner, Gerda (ed.). *Black Women in White America—A Documentary History*. New York: Pantheon Books, 1972.

Lincoln, C. Eric. *The Black Muslims in America*. Boston: Beacon Press, 1963.

Malcolm X. *The End of White World Supremacy—Four Speeches*. Edited by Benjamin Goodman. New York: Merlin House, Inc., 1971.

May, Edgar. *The Wasted Americans—Cost of Our Welfare Dilemma*. New York: Harper and Row, Publishers, 1964.

McKee, Ilse. *Tomorrow The World*. London: J. M. Dent and Sons Ltd., 1960.

McKissick, Floyd. *Three-Fifths of a Man*. New York: The Macmillan Co., 1969.

Mecklin, John Moffatt. *Democracy and Race Friction*. New York: The Macmillan Co., 1914.

Meek, Ronald L. *Marx and Engels on the Population Bomb*. Berkeley: The Ramparts Press, 1971.

Milio, Nancy. *9226 Kercheval—The Storefront That Did Not Burn*. Ann Arbor: University of Michigan Press—Ann Arbor Paperbacks, 1971.

Morgan, Robin (ed.). *Sisterhood Is Powerful—An Anthology of Writings from the Women's Liberation Movement*. New York: Vintage Books, 1970.

Muhammad, Elijah. *Message to the Blackman in America*. Chicago: Muhammad Mosque of Islam No. 2, 1965.

National Joint Action Committee. *The Black Woman—A Handbook* (n.p., March 1974).

*The Negro Family: The Case for National Action.* Office of Family Planning and Research, U.S. Department of Labor (March 1965). [The Moynihan Report]

Noonan, John T., Jr. *Contraception—A History of Its Treatment by the Catholic Theologians and Canonists.* New York: A Mentor-Omega Book, 1967.

Norton, Eleanor Holmes. *Population Growth and the Future of Black Folk.* PRB Selection No. 43, Washington, D.C.: Population Reference Bureau Inc., 1973.

Patterson, William L. (ed.) *We Charge Genocide—The Historic Petition to the United Nations for Relief from a Crime of the United States Government Against the Negro People.* New York: International Publishers, 1970.

Pinkney, Alphonso. *Black Americans.* Englewood Cliffs, N.J.: Prentice-Hall, Inc., 1969.

Popenoe, Paul, and Johnson, Roswell Hill. *Applied Eugenics.* New York: The Macmillan Co., 1918.

*Population and the American Future —The Report of the Commission on Population Growth and the American Future.* New York: New American Library, 1972.

Puckett, Newbell Niles. *Folk Beliefs of the Southern Negro.* New York: Negro Universities Press, 1968.

Rawick, George P. *From Sundown to Sunup—The Making of the Black Community.* Westport, Conn.: Greenwood Publishing Co., 1972.

Reid, Inez Smith. *"Together" Black Women.* New York: Emerson Hall Publishers, Inc. 1972.

Rice, Thurman B. *Racial Hygiene—A Practical Discussion of Eugenics and Race Culture.* New York: The Macmillan Co., 1929.

Sanders, Thomas G. *Opposition to Family Planning in Latin America: The Non-Marxist Left.* American Universities Field Staff Reports. West Coast South America Series XVII, No. 5 (March 1970).

——— *The Politics of Population in Brazil.* American Universities Field Staff Reports. East Coast South America Series XV, No. 1 (1971).

——— "The Relationship Between Population Planning and Belief Systems: The Catholic Church in Latin America." American Universities Field Staff Reports, Vol. 17, No. 7 (April 1970).

Sanger, Margaret. *Margaret Sanger: An Autobiography.* New York: W. W. Norton and Co. Publishers, 1938.

Sarvis, Betty, and Rodman, Hyman. *The Abortion Controversy.* New York: Columbia University Press, 1973.

Schulder, Diane, and Kennedy, Florynce. *Abortion Rap.* New York: McGraw-Hill Book Co., 1971.

Seaman, Barbara. *Free and Female.* New York: Coward, McCann and Geoghegan, 1972.

Sharp, Harry C. *The Sterilization of Degenerates.* Reprint of a paper read before the American Prison Association at Chicago, 1909.

Stycos, J. Mayone. *Ideology, Faith, and Family Planning in Latin America.* New York: McGraw-Hill Book Co., 1973.

Tannenbaum, Frank. *Slave and Citizen: The Negro in the Americas.* New York: Vintage Books, 1946.

*Thirty Years of Lynching in the United States 1889-1918.* New York: National Association for the Advancement of Colored People, 1919.

U.S. Commission on Population Growth and the American Future. *Statements at Public Hearings of the Commission on Population Growth and the American Future.* Volume VII of Commission Publications, Washington, D.C.: U.S. Government Printing Office, 1972.

Westoff, Charles F., and Westoff, Leslie Aldridge. *From Now to Zero: Fertility, Contraception and Abortion in America.* Boston: Little, Brown and Co., 1968.

Willhelm, Sidney H. *Who Needs The Negro?* Garden City, N.Y.: A Doubleday Anchor Book, 1971.

Williams, John A. *The Man Who Cried I Am.* Boston: Little, Brown and Co., 1967.

Williams, Maxine, and Newman, Pamela. *Black Women's Liberation.* New York: Pathfinder Press, Inc., 1970.

Willie, Charles V. "A Position Paper Presented to the President's Commission on Population Growth and the American Future," *Population Reference Bureau Selection,* No. 37, June 1971.

Woodside, Moya. *Sterilization in North Carolina: A Sociological and Psychological Study.* Chapel Hill: University of North Carolina Press, 1950.

Yetman, Norman R. *Life Under the "Peculiar Institution"—Selections from the Slave Narrative Collection.* New York: Holt, Rinehart and Winston Inc., 1970.

Yette, Samuel F. *The Choice: The Issue of Black Survival in America.* New York: G. P. Putnam's Sons, 1971.

Young, Whitney M., Jr. *To Be Equal.* New York: McGraw-Hill Book Co., 1964.


ARTICLES


Alexander, Daryl. "A Montgomery Tragedy." *Essence,* September 1973, pp. 42ff.

Alexander, Virginia M. "Contraception in Preventive Medicine." *Birth Control Review,* July-August 1932, pp. 215-216.

Alexander, W. G. "A Medical Viewpoint." *Birth Control Review,* June 1932, p. 175.

Alisky, Marvin. "Mexico Versus Malthus: National Trends." *Current History,* May 1974, pp. 200 ff.

Ashe, Christy. "Abortion or Genocide." *The Liberator,* August 1970, pp. 4-9.

Attah, Ernest B. "Racial Aspects of Zero Population Growth." *Science* 58 (15 June 1973), pp. 1143-1151.

Ayres, B. Drummond. "Sterilizing the Poor—Exploring Motives and Methods." *New York Times,* "News of the Week in Review," 8 July 1973, p. 4.

Bauman, Karl E., and Udry, J. Richard. "Powerlessness and Regularity of Contraception in an Urban Negro Male Sample: A Research Note." *Journal of Marriage and the Family* 34, No. 1 (February 1972): 112-114.

Beal, Frances M. "Double Jeopardy: To Be Black and Female." In *Sisterhood Is Powerful—An Anthology of Writings from the Women's Liberation Movement,* edited by Robin Morgan, pp. 340-353. New York: Vintage Books, 1970.

"Birth Control: Is It a Plan to Kill the Negro." *Hue,* July 1958, pp. 22-26.

Bishop, Jordan. "Imperialism and the Pill." *Commonweal,* 10 January 1969, pp. 465-467.

Bogue, Donald J. "Family Planning in the Negro Ghettos of Chicago."

*Milbank Memorial Fund Quarterly* 48, No. 2 (April 1970) Part 2: 283-299.

Bousfield, M. O. "Negro Public Health Work Needs Birth Control." *Birth Control Review*, June 1932, pp. 170-171.

Bradley, Valerie Jo. "Black Caucus Raps About Planned Genocide of Blacks." *Jet*, 6 August 1970, pp. 14-18.

Brooten, Gary. "The Birth Control Problem." *Evening Bulletin* (Philadelphia), 6, 7, 8 September 1967.

Bryant, Hilda. "Family Planning Center Here Wages Grim Social Struggle." *Seattle Post-Intelligencer* 15 December 1968, 34.

Buckhout, Robert. "Toward a Two-Child Norm: Changing Family Planning Attitudes." *American Psychologist* 27 (1972): 16-26.

Bull, Emily. "ACLU Planning to File Sterilization Suit." *Aiken Standard*, 15 April 1974.

Cade, Toni. "The Pill: Genocide or Liberation." In *The Black Woman: An Anthology*, edited by Toni Cade, pp. 162-169. New York: Signet Books, 1970.

Caldwell, Ben. "Top Secret or a Few Million After B.C." *The Drama Review* 12, No. 4 (Summer 1968): 47-50.

Campbell, Arthur A., and Kiser, Clyde V. "Nonwhite Fertility and Family Planning." In *The Biological and Social Meaning of Race*, edited by Richard H. Osborne, pp. 135-148. San Francisco: W. H. Freeman and Company, 1971.

Carter, Elmer A. "Eugenics for the Negro." *Birth Control Review*, 16, June 1932, pp. 169-170.

Chasteen, Edgar. "The Stork Is Not the Bird of Paradise." Reprinted from *Mademoiselle Magazine*, January 1970.

Cobb, W. Montague. "The Negro As a Biological Element in the American Population." *Journal of Negro Education* 8, No. 3 (July 1939): 336-348.

Coburn, Judith. "Sterilization Regulations: Debate Not Quelled by HEW Document." *Science*, 8 March 1974, pp. 935-939.

Coleman, Marsha. "Are Abortions for Black Women Racist?" *The Militant*, 21 January 1972, p. 19.

"Conversation: Jesse Jackson and Marcia Gillespie." *Essence*, July 1971, pp. 24-27.

Cooper, George M. "Birth Control in the North Carolina Health

Department.'' *North Carolina Medical Journal* 1, No. 9 (September 1940): 463-468.

Corey, Marsha. ''The State of Organized Family Planning Programs in the United States, 1973.'' *Family Planning Perspectives* 6, No. 1 (Winter 1974): 15-26.

Corkey, Elizabeth C. ''A Family Planning Program for the Low-Income Family.'' *Journal of Marriage and the Family*, November 1964, pp. 478-480.

Curvin, Robert. ''Black Power in City Hall.'' *Society*, September-October 1972, pp. 55-58.

Du Bois, W. E. B. ''Birth.'' *The Crisis* 24 (October 1922): 248-250.

———''Black Folk and Birth Control.'' *Birth Control Review* 16 (June 1932): 166-167.

Ehrlich, Paul R., and Ehrlich, Anne H. ''Population Control and Genocide.'' *New Democratic Coalition Newsletter*, July 1970, p. 5.

———, and Holdren, John P. ''Who Makes the Babies.'' *Saturday Review*, 6 February 1971, p. 60.

Eliot, Johan W.; Hall, Robert E.; Willson, Robert; and Houser, Carolyn. ''The Obstetrician's View.'' In *Abortion in a Changing World*, edited by Robert E. Hall, Vol. 1, pp. 85-95. New York: Columbia University Press, 1970.

Farley, Reynolds. ''Indications of Recent Demographic Change Among Blacks.'' *Social Biology* 18, No. 4 (December 1971): 341-358.

Farrakhan, Minister Louis. ''The Black Woman.'' *Essence*, January 1972, pp. 30 ff.

''Feminism 'The Black Nuance'.'' *Newsweek*, 17 December 1973, pp. 89-90.

Fenston, Joy. ''Opposition Kills Sterilization Bill; Slave Labor Bill Lives.'' *Muhammad Speaks*, 30 April 1971.

Ferebee, Dorothy Boulding. ''Planned Parenthood As a Public Health Measure for the Negro Race.'' *Human Fertility* 7, No. 1 (February 1942): 7-10.

Ferster, Elyce Zenoff. ''Eliminating the Unfit—Is Sterilization the Answer?'' *Ohio State Law Journal* 27 (1966): 591-633.

Fischer, Constance. ''The Negro Social Worker Evaluates Birth Control.'' *Birth Control Review*, June 1932, pp. 174-175.

Frazier, E. Franklin. "Birth Control for *More Negro Babies.*" *Negro Digest* 3 (July 1945): 41-44.

———"The Negro and Birth Control." *Birth Control Review*, March 1933, pp. 68-70.

———"Eugenics and the Race Problem." *The Crisis* 31 (December 1925): 91-92.

Furstenburg, Frank F. "Attitudes Toward Abortion Among Young Blacks." *Studies in Family Planning* 3, No. 4 (April 1972): 66-69.

———"Premarital Pregnancy Among Black Teenagers." *Trans-Action*, May 1970, pp. 52-55.

Garvin, Charles H. "The Negro Doctor's Task." *Birth Control Review*, November 1932, pp. 269-270.

Gold, Edwin M; Erhardt, Carl L.; Jacobziner, Harold; and Nelson, Frieda. "Therapeutic Abortions in New York City: A 20-Year Review." *American Journal of Public Health* 55, No. 7 (July 1965): 964-972.

Gray, Naomi. "Blacks Question Zero Population Growth as Goal." *Internal Medicine News*, 1 June 1971, p. 1.

———"How to Work Effectively with the Poor." *Planned Parenthood—World Population*, 5 October 1966, pp. 1-11.

Greer, Edward. "The 'Liberation' of Gary, Indiana." *Trans-Action* 8, No. 3 (January 1971): 38-39, 63.

Gregory, Dick. "My Answer to Genocide." *Ebony*, October 1971, pp. 66 ff.

Gullattee, Alyce M. "The Politics of Eugenics ." In *Eugenic Sterilization*, edited by Jonas Robitscher, pp. 82-93. Springfield, Ill.: Charles C Thomas Publisher, 1973.

Hall, Robert E. "Abortion in American Hospitals." *American Journal of Public Health* 57, No. 11 (November 1967): 1933-1936.

Hare, Nathan. "Black Ecology." *The Black Scholar* 1 (April 1970): 2-8.

Hellman, Louis. "One Galileo Is Enough: Some Aspects of Current Population Problems." *The Eugenics Review* 57, No. 4 (December 1965): 161-166.

Hill, Adelaide Cromwell, and Jaffe, Frederick S. "Negro Fertility and Family Size Preferences: Implications for Programming of Health and Social Services." In *The Negro American*, edited by Talcott Parsons and Kenneth B. Clark, pp. 205-224. Boston: Beacon Press, 1967.

Holmes, S. J. "The Negro Birth Rate." *Birth Control Review*, June 1932, pp. 172-173.

Holzer, Marc. "ZPG: A Jewish Concern." *Congress Bi-Weekly*, 9 November 1973, pp. 12-14.

Hudgins, John. "Is Birth Control Genocide?" *The Black Scholar* 4, No. 3 (November-December 1972): 34-37.

Hughes, Langston. "Population Explosion." *New York Post*, 10 December 1965.

"Illegitimate Plan." *The Providence Evening Bulletin*, 7 November, 1971.

"International Planned Parenthood Federation: Survey of Member Organizations." *Studies in Family Planning*, No. 17 (February 1967), pp. 13-16.

"Is Birth Control a Menace? To Negroes." *Jet*, 19 August 1954, pp. 53-55.

Jaffe, Frederick S. "Family Planning, Public Policy and Intervention Strategy." *Journal of Social Issues* 23, No. 4 (July 1967): 145-163.

————"Low-Income Families: Fertility Changes in the 1960's." *Family Planning Perspectives* 4 (January 1972): 43-47.

———— "Low-Income Families: Fertility in 1971-1972." *Family Planning Perspectives* 6, No. 2 (Spring 1974): 108-110.

————, and Polgar, Steven. "Family Planning and Public Policy: Is the 'Culture of Poverty' the New Cop-Out?" *Journal of Marriage and the Family* 30, No. 2 (May 1968): 228-235.

Johnson, Charles S. "A Question of Negro Health." *Birth Control Review*, June 1932, 167-169.

Jones, Carolyn. "Abortion and Black Women." *Black America*, No. 5 (September 1970): 48-49.

Jordan, Vernon, Jr., "Census Bureau May Have Missed You." *New York Amsterdam News*, 8 September 1973.

————, "To Be Equal—Sterilization Scandal Shows Experimenters Still Busy." *Afro-American*, 28 July 1973, p. 4.

Kahlil, Brother. "Eugenics, Birth Control and the Black Man." *Black News*, 14 January 1971, pp. 20-21.

Kahn, E. J., Jr. "A Reporter at Large—Who, What, Where, How Much, How Many?" Part II. *The New Yorker*, 22 October 1973, pp. 105 ff.

Kandell, Jonathan. "Argentina, Hoping to Double Her Population This

Century, Is Taking Action to Restrict Birth Control." *New York Times*, 17 March 1974, p. 4.

Kantor, William M. "Beginnings of Sterilization in America." *Journal of Heredity* 28, No. 11 (November 1937): 374-376.

Kennard, Gail. "Sterilization Abuse." *Essence*, October 1974, pp. 66 ff.

Kiser, Clyde V. "Fertility of Harlem Negroes." *Milbank Memorial Fund Quarterly* 13, No. 3 (July 1935): 272-285.

————, and Frank, Myrna E. "Factors Associated with the Low Fertility of Nonwhite Women of College Attainment." *Milbank Memorial Fund Quarterly* 45, No. 4 (October 1967): 427-449.

LaRue, Linda. "The Black Movement and Women's Liberation." Reprinted from *The Black Scholar* (May 1970): 2-8.

Lear, Len. " '5 Days of Agony and Then a Lifetime of Joy,' Says Prominent Advocate of Male Sterilization." *Philadelphia Tribune*, 15 July 1972.

Lees, Hannah. "The Negro Response to Birth Control." *The Reporter*, 19 May 1966, pp. 46-48.

Leifermann, Henry. "They Still Think Sterilization Is Good Enough for Welfare Mothers." *Southern Voices* 1, No. 2 (May-June 1974): 79-81.

Lelyveld, Joseph. "Family Planning in Louisiana." *New York Times Magazine*, 19 July 1970, pp. 24-34.

Lester, Julius. "Birth Control and Blacks." In *Revolutionary Notes*, pp. 140-143. New York: Richard W. Baron, 1969.

Lewis, Julian. "Can the Negro Afford Birth Control." *Negro Digest* 3 (May 1945): 19-22.

Lincoln, Richard. "S2108: Capitol Hill Debates the Future of Population and Family Planning." *Family Planning Perspectives* 2, No. 1 (January 1970): 6-12.

Lipson, Gerald, and Wolman, Dianne. "Polling Americans on Birth Control and Population." *Family Planning Perspectives* 4 (January 1972): 39-42.

Ludlow, Charles. "Truth About Sterilization." *Dawn Magazine*, October 1973, pp. 21-22.

Miller, Kelly. "Eugenics of the Negro Race." *The Scientific Monthly* 5 (July 1917): 57-59.

Monroe, Keith. "How California's Abortion Law Isn't Working." *New York Times Magazine*, 29 December 1968, pp. 10-20.

Morrison, Joseph L. "Illegitimacy, Sterilization, and Racism: A North Carolina Case History." *Social Service Review* 29, No. 1 (March 1965): 1-10.

O'Connor, John J. "TV: Shockley versus Innis." *New York Times*, 13 December 1973.

Pakter, Jean; O'Hare, Donna; Nelson, Frieda; and Svigar, Martin. "Two Years Experience in New York City with the Liberalized Abortion Law—Progress and Problems." *American Journal of Public Health* 63, No. 6 (June 1973): 524-535.

Partington, Donald H. "The Incidence of the Death Penalty for Rape in Virginia." *Washington and Lee Review* 22 (1965): 43-75.

Paul, Julius. "The Return of Punitive Sterilization Proposals: Current Attacks on Illegitimacy and the AFDC Program." *Law and Society Review* 3, No. 1 (August 1968): 77-106.

————"State Eugenic Sterilization History: A Brief Overview." In *Eugenic Sterilization*, edited by Jonas Robitscher. pp. 25-40. Springfield, Ill.: Charles C Thomas Publisher, 1973.

Payne, Ethel. "Women in Politics." *Dawn Magazine*, October 1973, pp. 4 ff.

Pearl, Raymond. "Fertility and Contraception in Urban Whites and Negroes." *Science* 83 (22 May 1936): 503-506.

"Planned Parenthood." *The Crisis* 77, No. 3 (March 1970): 78-79.

Planning Unit Center for Family Planning Program Development. "The Need for Family Planning Services in the United States, 1974." *Family Planning Perspectives* 6, No. 1 (Winter 1974): 27-29.

Pope, Carl. "Washington Report." *ZPG National Reporter*, November-December 1971, p. 14.

Popenoe, Paul. "The Progress of Eugenic Sterilization." *Journal of Heredity* 25, No. 1 (January 1934): 19-26.

Raspberry, William. "Classicide—Sterilization Is the New Social Work." *Philadelphia Inquirer*, 27 July 1973.

Rivers, Eunice; Shuman, Stanley H.; Simpson, Lloyd; and Olansky, Sidney. "Twenty Years of Followup Experience in a Long-Range Medical Study." *Public Health Reports* 68, No. 4 (April 1953): 391-392.

Rodriguez, Walter. "Family Planning: Hope for a Nation." In *Population and Family Planning in Latin America*, Report #17. Washington, D.C.: Victor Bostrom Fund, 1973: pp. 20-22.

Rowan, Carl. "U.S. Family Planning Progress." *Scrantonian*, 28, March 1971.

Rutledge, Al. "Is Abortion Black Genocide?" *Essence*, September 1973, pp. 36 ff.

Sanger, Margaret. "The Case for Birth Control." *The Crisis* 41, No. 6 (June 1934): 176-177.

Sauer, R. "Attitudes to Abortion in America 1800-1973." *Population Studies* 28, No. 1 (March 1974): 53-67.

Schuyler, George S. "Quantity or Quality." *Birth Control Review*, 16 June 1932, pp. 165-166.

Segal, Aaron. "Too Much of a Good Thing." *Caribbean Review* 5 No. 4 (October, November, December 1973): 37-40.

Seibels, Robert E. "A Rural Project in Negro Material Health." *Human Fertility* 6, No. 2 (April 1941): 42-44.

Sharp, Harry C. "Vasectomy As a Means of Preventing Procreation in Defectives." *Journal of the American Medical Association* 53, No. 23 (1909): 1897-1902.

Shockley, William. "Dysgenics, Geneticity, Raceology: A Challenge To The Intellectual Responsibility of Educators." A Special Supplement of the *Phi Delta Kappan* (January 1972): 297-307.

Sims, Newell L. "Hostages to the White Man." *Birth Control Review* (July-August 1932): 214-215.

Sinnette, Calvin H. "Genocide and Black Ecology" *Freedomways*, 12 No. 1 (1972): 34-46.

Sklar, June and Berkov, Beth. "The Effects of Legal Abortions on Legitimate and Illegitimate Birth Rates: The California Experience." *Studies in Family Planning*, 4, No. 11 (November 1973): 281-292.

Slater, Jack. "Condemmed to Die for Science." *Ebony*, November 1972, pp. 177 ff.

Smith, Mary. "Birth Control and the Negro Woman." *Ebony*, March 1968, pp. 29 ff.

Staples, Robert. "Research on Black Sexuality: Its Implication for

Family Life, Sex Education, and Public Policy.'' *The Family Coordinator*, 21, No. 2 (April 1972): 183-188.

————''The Myth of the Black Matriarchy.'' *The Black Scholar* (February 1970): 2-10.

''Sterilization Guidelines: 22 Months on the Shelf.'' *Medical World News* 9 November 1973, pp. 53 ff.

''Stresses and Strains on Black Women.'' *Ebony*, June 1974, pp. 33 ff.

Stycos, J. Mayone. ''Public and Private Opinions on Population and Family Planning.'' *Studies in Family Planning*, No. 51 (March 1970): 10-17.

———— ''Opposition to Family Planning in Latin America: Conservative Nationalism,'' *Demography*, 5, No. 2 (1968): 846-854.

Sweet, James A. ''Differentials in the Rate of Fertility Decline 1960-1970.'' *Family Planning Perspectives*, 6 No. 2 (Spring 1974): 103-107.

Sutin, Kathie. ''1.5 M. U.S. Jews Lost by ZPG Since 1940.'' *The Jewish Post and Opinion*, 19 April 1974, p. 1.

Tendler, Moses D. ''Population Control—The Jewish View:'' *Tradition* 8, No. 3 (fall 1966): 5-14.

Terpenning, Walter A. ''God's Chillun.'' *Birth Control Review*, June 1932, pp. 171-172.

Tietze, Christopher, and Lewit, Sarah. ''Patterns of Family Limitation in a Rural Negro Community.'' *American Sociological Review* 18, No. 5 (October 1953): 563-564.

Treadwell, Mary. ''Is Abortion Black Genocide?'' *Family Planning Perspectives* 4, No. 1 (January 1972): 4-5.

Turner, Castellano B., and Darity, William A. ''Fears of Genocide Among Black Americans As Related to Age, Sex, and Region.'' *American Journal of Public Health* 63, No. 12 (December 1973): 1029-1034.

Valien, Preston, and Fitzgerald, Alberta Price. ''Attitudes of the Negro Mother Toward Birth Control.'' *American Journal of Sociology* 55 (November 1949): 279-283.

————, and Vaughn, Ruth E. ''Birth Control Attitudes and Practices of Negro Mothers.'' *Sociology And Social Research* 35, No. 6 (July-August 1951): 415-421.

Varky, George, and Dean, Charles R. ''Planned Parenthood Patients:

Black and White." *Family Planning Perspectives* 2, No. 1 (January 1970): 34-37.

Walters, Ronald. "Population Control and the Black Community." Part I. *The Black Scholar* 5, No. 8 (May 1974): 45-51.

————"Population Control and the Black Community." Part II. *The Black Scholar* 5, No. 9 (June 1974): 25-31.

Watts, Daniel H. "Birth Control." *Liberator*, May 1969, p. 3.

"Watts Extended Health and Family Planning Group Inc." *The Family Planner*, December 1969, pp. 4-5.

Welsing, Frances C. "On Black Genetic Inferiority." *Ebony*, July 1974, pp. 104-105.

Westhoff, Charles F. "The Modernization of U.S. Contraceptive Practice." *Family Planning Perspectives* 4, No. 3 (July 1972): 9-12.

Westoff, Leslie Aldridge. "Sterilization." *New York Times Magazine*, 29 September 1974, pp. 30 ff.

Wilkins, Roy. "Wilkins Speaks—Dodging Census Taker Can Cost Your Children Money." *Afro-American*, 15 December 1973.

Wolfers, David, and Wolfers, Helen. "Vasectomania." *Family Planning Perspectives* 5, No. 4 (Fall 1973): 196-199.

Wolfgang, Marvin, and Riedel, Marc. "Race, Judicial Discretion and the Death Penalty." *Annals of the American Academy of Political and Social Science* 407 (May 1973): 119-133.

"ZPG: A Fascist Movement: A Progressive Labor Party Position." *The American Population Debate*, edited by Daniel Callahan. Garden City, N.Y.: Doubleday Anchor Books, 1971.


NEWSPAPERS AND PERIODICALS. SPECIFIC ARTICLES ARE CITED UNDER "ARTICLES."


*Advocate-News* [Barbados], 5 September 1972; 7 September 1972; 9 January 1973; 7 May 1973

*Afro-American*, 21 July 1973; 28 July 1973; 11 August 1973

*Amsterdam News*, 21 July 1973

*Augusta Chronicle*, 25 May 1966

*The Black Man*, November 1934

*The Black Panther*, 4 January 1969; 4 July 1970; 10 April 1971; 8 May
    1971; 7 July 1973; 14 July 1973; 11 August 1973
*The* [Toledo] *Blade*, 19 April 1973
*Boston Globe*, 29 April 1972
*Chicago Daily Defender*, 25 July 1973
*Cincinnati Post and Times Star*, 25 April 1973
*Congressional Record*, 5 February 1974, S1265
*Daily Challenge*, 17 July 1973
*Detroit Free Press*, 27 November 1970; 6 December 1973
*Jet*, 17 August 1972
*Journal of the American Medical Association*, 21 December 1964
*Los Angeles Times*, 30 September 1968
*The Militant*, 16 March 1973
*Muhammad Speaks*, 9 July 1965; 16 July 1965; 23 July 1965; 11 October
    1968; 24 January 1969; 14 March 1969; 23 May 1969; 31 May
    1969; 4 July 1969; 11 July 1969; 29 August 1969; 5 December
    1969; 26 December 1969; 22 November 1970; 3 January 1971; 13
    July 1973; 27 July 1973; 24 August 1973
*Newsweek*, 12 June 1972
*New York Post*, 7 October 1968
*New York Times*, 1967-1974
*Overseas Express* [Trinidad], 17 September 1973
*The Philadelphia Evening Bulletin*, 20 December 1965
*The Philadelphia Inquirer*, 20 June 1966
*The Pittsburgh Catholic*, 21 February 1969
*Pittsburgh Courier*, 29 March 1947; 14 April 1947; 24 August 1968
*Pittsburgh Press*, 15 August 1968; 21 August 1968
*Planned Parenthood—World Population Washington Memo*, 1973-
    1974
*The* [Cleveland] *Plain Dealer*, 20 April 1973
*Providence Journal*, 7 June 1970
*Providence Sunday Journal*, 24 March 1974
*Roanoke, Virginia Times*, 22 July 1973
*San Francisco Chronicle*, 9 June 1966
*Springfield Sunday Republican*, 7 June 1970
*The* [Kingston, Jamaica] *Star*, 8 February 1968
*The Thunderbolt*, June 1971

*United States Department of Commerce News*, 25 April 1973; 11 January 1974
*Washington Post*, 27 January 1965; 25 May 1966; 24 July 1973
*The Washington Star*, 22 September 1967
*The Wilmington News*, 16 November 1962
*Yale News*, 27 January 1972

## UNPUBLISHED WORKS

Attah, Ernest B. "Racial Aspects of Zero Population Growth: Some Perspectives with Demographic Models." A paper prepared for presentation to the Population Association of America, April 1972.

Berry, Edwin C. "The Negro, Poverty and Population." Address delivered at the Planned Parenthood World Population National Conference in Milwaukee, 7 May 1965.

Darity, William A.; Turner, Castellano B.; and Thiebaux, H. Jean. "Race Consciousness and Fears of Black Genocide As Barriers to Family Planning." Paper presented at the Ninth Annual Meeting of the American Association of Planned Parenthood Physicians, Kansas City, Mo., 5,6 April 1971.

Darney, P. D. "A Statewide Family Planning Program's Effect on Fertility." Paper presented at the annual meeting of the Population Association of America, New Orleans, La., 27 April 1973.

"Genocide," Position statement presented by the Black Caucus. First National Congress on Optimum Population and Environment, 7-11 June 1970.

Jaffe, Frederick S. "Family Planning Services in the United States." Prepared for the Commission on Population Growth and the American Future.

Moore, Emily C. "Native American Indian Values: Their Relation to Suggested Population Policy Proposals." Unpublished paper prepared for the Population Task Force of the Institute for Society, Ethics, and the Life Sciences as part of its study for the Commission on Population Growth and the American Future, n.d.

Murray, Robert F., Jr. "The Ethical and Moral Values of Black Americans and Population Policy." Unpublished paper prepared for the Population Task Force of the Institute of Society, Ethics, and the Life Sciences as part of its study for the Commission on Population Growth and the American Future.

O'Boyle, Archbishop Patrick A. "Sterilization and the Medically Indigent." Sermon delivered in St. Matthew's Cathedral, Washington, D.C. 9 September 1962.

Policy statement approved by the National Urban League's Board of Trustees. 19 November 1962.

Rosenfeld, Bernard; Wolfe, Sidney M.; and McGarrah, Robert E., Jr. "A Health Research Group Study on Surgical Sterilization: Present Abuses and Proposed Regulations." Unpublished report, 29 October 1973.

Smith, Robert Henderson. "Family Planning and Contraceptive Practices As Related to Social Class Membership of Black Families." Ph.D. dissertation, Florida State University, 1973.

Speech by Floyd McKissick to the Liturgical Conference, Park Sheraton Hotel, Washington, D.C., 20 August 1968.

Stycos, J. Mayone. "Some Minority Opinions on Birth Control: Blacks, Women's Liberation, and the New Left." Unpublished paper prepared for the Population Task Force of the Institute of Society, Ethics, and the Life Sciences as part of its study for the Commission on Population Growth and the American Future, June 1971.

Warwick, Donald P. and Williamson, Nancy. "Population Policy and Spanish Speaking Americans." Unpublished paper prepared for the Population Task Force of the Institute for Society, Ethics, and the Life Sciences as part of its study for the Commission on Population Growth and the American Future, August 1971.

PERSONAL INTERVIEWS

Innis, Roy. Personal interview with the author, Kingston, R.I. 17 May 1972

Means, Russell. Personal interview with the author. Kingston, R.I. 11 May 1974.

Walcott, Colonel O.F.C., President of the Barbados Family Planning Association. Personal interview with the author. Bridgetown, Barbados. 4 April 1973.

# Index